Drawings of People by the

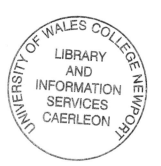

To Amelia Fysh (née Bullen)

Drawings of People by the Under-5s

Maureen Cox

Falmer Press

UK   The Falmer Press, 1 Gunpowder Square, London, EC4A 3DE
USA The Falmer Press, Taylor & Francis Inc., 1900 Frost Road, Suite 101, Bristol, PA 19007

First published in 1997

A catologue record for this book is available from the British Library

Library of Congress Catologing-in-Publication Data are available on request

ISBN 0 7507 0584 1 paper

Jacket design by Caroline Archer
Design by Carla Turchini

Printed by Graphicraft Typesetters Ltd., Hong Kong

Contents

Acknowledgments

Figures

Note: 'AF' in the figure captions throughout this book refers to the Amelia Fysh collection of children's human figure drawings (see pages 104–106 for further details).

Figures 1 and 13 are taken from Major, D.R. (1906) *First Steps in Mental Growth*. New York: MacMillan.

Figures 2 and 3 are taken from Kellogg, R. (1970) *Analyzing Children's Art*. Palo Alto, Calif.: Mayfield.

The owner and copyright holder of the drawings in Figures 4, 48, 71, 72, 73, 74 and 80 is Dr Maureen Cox.

Amelia Fysh is the owner and copyright holder of Figures 5, 6, 7, 8, 9, 10, 11, 14, 15, 16, 18, 19, 20, 21, 22, 24, 25, 27, 28, 29, 30, 31, 32, 33, 34, 35, 36, 37, 39, 40, 41, 42, 43, 44, 45, 46, 47, 50, 52, 54, 55, 56, 57, 58, 59, 60, 61, 62, 63, 64, 65, 66, and 67. Printed with permission.

Figure 12 is taken from Ricci, C. (1887) *L'Arte dei Bambini*. Bologna: N. Zanichelli.

Nikki Pitchford collected the drawing in Figure 17; the owner and copyright holder is Dr Maureen Cox.

Figure 23 is taken from Arnheim, R. (1974) *Art and Visual Perception: A Psychology of the Creative Eye. The New Version*. 2nd edition. Berkeley, Los Angeles: University of California Press. Reprinted with permission.

Figure 26 is taken from Goodnow, J. (1977) *Children's Drawing*. London: Fontana/Open Books. Reprinted with permission.

Figure 38 is taken from Eng, H. (1931) *The Psychology of Children's Drawings*. London: Routledge & Kegan Paul.

Rachel Moore collected the drawing in Figure 49 and this was first published in Cox, M.V. and Moore, R. (1994) Children's depictions of different views of the human figure. *Educational Psychology*, 14, pp. 427-436.

Figure 51 is taken from Goodenough, F. (1926) *Measurement of Intelligence by Drawings*. New York: Harcourt, Brace & World.

Claire Howarth collected the drawing in Figure 53 and this was first published in Cox, M.V. and Howarth, C. (1989) The human figure drawings of normal children and those with severe learning difficulties. *British Journal of Developmental Psychology*, 7, pp. 333-339.

Figures 68 and 69 are drawn from an article by Andrew Wilson in *Top Santé Magazine*, September 1993.

Professor Tu Mei Ru provided the Chinese art textbook from which Figure 70 was taken.

Sarah Mason collected the drawings in Figures 75 and 76.

Gayle Ridge collected the drawings in Figures 77, 78 and 79; the owner and copyright holder is Dr Maureen Cox.

Grant Cooke drew the cartoon in Figure 81 and this was first published in Cox, M., Cooke, G. and Griffin, D. (1995) Teaching children to draw in the infants school. *Journal of Art & Design Education*, 14, pp. 153-163.

Figures 82 and 83 contain drawings completed by children in a project entitled *The Teaching of Drawing in the Infants School: An Evaluation of the 'Negotiated Drawing' Method* which was funded by the Leverhulme Trust and directed by Dr Maureen Cox.

Plates

Plate 1. Dr John Matthews provided the photograph of his son Ben.

Plates 2a–c. Rosemary Hill provided the Australian Aboriginal children's drawings. I also acknowledge the Warlpiri Media Association and thank the people of Yuendumu, Central Australia.

Plates 3a & b. Dr Kai On Li provided the photographs of the Chinese children's artwork produced in Jilin City, People's Republic of China.

Plate 4. Amelia Fysh provided this photograph of herself and children at Beech Green Nursery.

Plate 1 An action representation by Ben, aged 2 years 1 month.

Drawings of people by the under-5s: an introduction

Drawing and painting are activities that form an important part of pre-school education. In fact, most children actually do far more drawing than painting since pencils, crayons and felt-tipped pens (or magic markers, as some people call them) are more readily at hand and are far less messy, an important consideration for many parents. Most children really enjoy drawing and adults find their pictures charming and often amusing. But, at the same time, we are often amazed and bewildered by the world revealed in young children's pictures. Their figures seem to have extraordinarily large heads, the arms may stick out from the sides of the head and there often appears to be no body at all. Parents may wonder if their children are normal or if there is something dreadfully wrong with them.

If we look carefully at children's drawings throughout the pre-school period we can discover what normal development is actually like. In this book I shall begin this exploration from the time children start to attend play groups or nurseries – usually at a time when they are still scribbling – to the end of the pre-school when most children will be able to draw a variety of recognizable objects including the human figure. I shall, in fact, concentrate on their depiction of the human figure since this is one of the earliest recognizable things that children draw and, not surprisingly, it remains a popular topic throughout their schooldays, whether drawn on its own or as part of a more complex scene.

I shall introduce some of the ideas and explanations that various researchers have put forward to account for the curious ways in which the human figure is drawn, but I shall also be critical of these ideas. I am aware that some readers may be rather dismissive about research, perhaps feeling that it is a bit remote and that their own experience of looking at drawings is more important. But Victoria Hurst (1991) thinks that this would be a pity: 'There is an understandable feeling that research is too rarefied for the daily business of looking after children – that its conclusions are better suited to the readers of learned journals than to Nursery teachers and Nursery nurses. But is this really true? Can we afford for it to be so?' (p. 141). Indeed, I don't think that the conclusions from research studies are only for learned journals; on the contrary, they should and do feed back into our daily lives, helping us to have a better understanding of what is going on. But for those readers who may still feel sceptical, rest assured that in this book I shall not move very far away from observing the children's drawings themselves and shall use them as illustrative examples as much as possible.

I have been carrying out research for over fifteen years on the drawings produced by hundreds of children ranging in age from only one year right up to adulthood. In most cases I have only one drawing per child but, because there are so many children at each

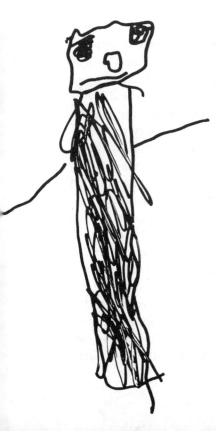

age level, we can get an idea of the changes in development over the whole childhood period. This kind of research is called 'cross-sectional' for the simple reason that we take a sample of the work of a cross-section of children at each age. The information is very useful in that we can see what kinds of drawings children at different ages are producing. But it is also limited since we cannot see a developmental pattern for an *individual* child and we can only infer from the cross-sectional data what any particular child's development might be like. The kind of research which traces individual children over a period of time is not so common because it is much more time-consuming and more expensive to carry out. So, there are far fewer 'longitudinal' studies in the research literature and many of these are case studies of just one child, usually the researcher's own son or daughter.

In fact I also have a series of drawings produced by my own daughter. I collected the vast majority of the drawings she produced both at home and at nursery right from the time she began to scribble. I also have sets of drawings made by five other children who attended her nursery: the sets start when these children were still scribbling and follow them through a one-year period until they were all drawing recognizable figures. This longitudinal study of six pre-school children by Cox and Parkin was published in 1986. More recently, I have been fortunate enough to study a very special collection of figure drawings compiled by a nursery school head teacher, Amelia Fysh (*see Plate 4 and pp. 104 – 106 for further details of Amelia Fysh and her collection*). From time to time, Amelia would ask her children to draw a man or a lady so that she could put the picture in her special folder. Each figure was dated and, when the child left the nursery, the set was mounted so that we can see more easily the developmental sequence. Some of the children were also contacted much later in their primary school years; a few examples of these later drawings of 'My family' are included in this book (*see Figures 24, 34, 35, 47, 52 and 62*). In total there are sets of drawings from 299 children, which represent a particularly valuable resource for teachers and researchers interested in children's early attempts to draw. It is the fact that the sets are longitudinal – that they follow the same child over a period of time – that is so important. Another notable feature of the collection is that some of the children had special needs – they had physical or intellectual disabilities or learning difficulties – and some came from difficult or deprived home backgrounds.

1

Scribbling

Although many nurseries can accommodate very young babies, most take children from about the age of 2 or 2 years 6 months. By this age most children have had at least some experience of using a pencil, crayons or felt-tipped pens. Of course, many children will still be scribbling and may not produce anything recognizable for quite some time. Unfortunately many parents and teachers seem to regard scribbling in a rather negative way. The educational psychologist Sir Cyril Burt (1921) thought of it largely in terms of motor movements without any particular purpose. This is a pity since, in fact, there is more to it than this and we may also see some development taking place within this scribbling 'stage'. So, it is a mistake to dismiss it as 'just scribbling'.

Like Cyril Burt, some other early writers (e.g., Bender, 1938; Harris, 1963) recognized that scribbling is an enjoyable activity for children primarily because of the rhythmic movement of the arm. As early as 1906, D.R. Major traced the development of scribbling in his son 'R'. Around the time of his first birthday R would strike the paper with a pencil, a spoon or any similar implement, apparently in imitation of an adult's drawing or writing (*see Figure 1*). Gradually the arm movements became freer and the random disconnected lines produced with a pencil gave way to a more rhythmic left-to-right or back-and-forth motion of the hand, producing slightly curved lines with a loop at the end of each one. Those produced with the right hand dipped down towards the left and those with the left hand dipped down towards the right (*see middle section of Figure 1*). This swinging motion became more purposive and under good control by the time R was 18 months old.

From 18 months R began to add other movements: as well as horizontal lines often returning upon themselves he produced up-and-down and round-and-round scribbles (*see scribble produced at*

Figure 1: Tentative stabs at the paper at 12 months of age give way to freer, rhythmic movements at 16 months. Round-and-round scribbles become more controlled by age 2 years.

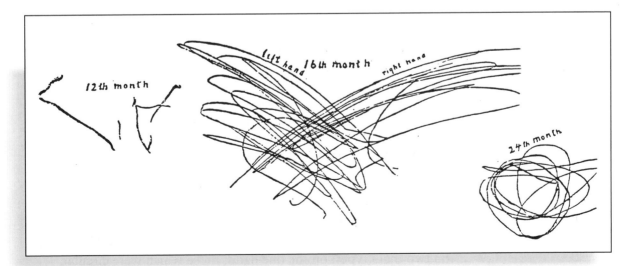

24 months in Figure 1). R's round-and-round scribbles became more controlled until he could produce an irregularly shaped figure bearing some resemblance to a circle or an oval.

Other researchers too have reported the increasing control that children manage to gain over the pencil and their ability to curtail their loopy or spiralling scribbles in order to form a roughly circular closed form (e.g., Bender, 1938; Piaget and Inhelder, 1956). This is important according to Rudolf Arnheim (1974) because the enclosed shape seems to suggest a figure against a background and opens up quite staggering possibilities of representation. By placing dots or scribbles within or outside the shape the child can represent important spatial relationships between objects or parts of an object. For example, a figure's eyes, nose and mouth can be contained *within* the boundary of the face. In Figure 23 two fish are contained *within* the boundary of the house in the centre of the picture.

Rhoda Kellogg (1970) amassed a huge collection of children's scribbles and claimed to have discovered twenty different basic types, although each individual child doesn't necessarily produce all twenty of them (*see Figure 2*). She said that after practising these basic scribbles children then start to combine them and make more complicated forms. For example, they might draw a cross with two diagonal strokes; Kellogg called this a 'diagram'. Framed inside a circle or a square it becomes a 'combine'. A figure composed of three or more diagrams is an 'aggregate'. These figures are elaborated into 'mandalas' (*see level 3 of Figure 3*). Then, at a later stage, 'sun schemas' appear – circular shapes and patterns with lines radiating from them (*see level 4 of Figure 3*). These sun schemas in turn are adapted, mainly with a face being added, and become the first representations of people. The idea, then, is of a progressive development from a repertoire of simple scribbles which are combined and recombined by the child into more complex patterns (*see Figure 3*). Although Rhoda Kellogg was careful to say that not all children necessarily go through all the steps in this process she none the less gave the impression of an orderly, step-by-step progression.

Now, we can sometimes see different kinds of scribbles used by different children in the nursery and one individual child may use a variety of types of scribble. But what evidence is there that the scribbles can be classified into twenty different types, as Rhoda Kellogg claimed? Well, the evidence is not very strong at all. Claire Golomb and Linda Whitaker tried to identify all these different scribbles (Golomb, 1981) in a study of 250 children. These researchers and their colleagues had great difficulty in agreeing with each other about the scribbles and, in the end, they could only agree on two main types: on the one hand, those which were circular,

Figure 2: *(right)* Twenty different basic scribbles identified by Rhoda Kellogg.

Figure 3: *(bottom)* According to Kellogg, basic scribbles are combined and recombined into more elaborate units.

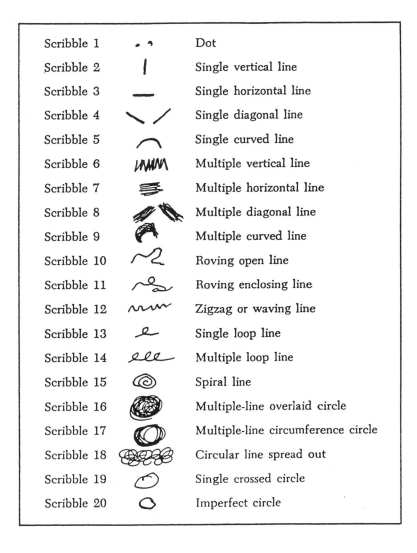

Scribble 1		Dot
Scribble 2		Single vertical line
Scribble 3		Single horizontal line
Scribble 4		Single diagonal line
Scribble 5		Single curved line
Scribble 6		Multiple vertical line
Scribble 7		Multiple horizontal line
Scribble 8		Multiple diagonal line
Scribble 9		Multiple curved line
Scribble 10		Roving open line
Scribble 11		Roving enclosing line
Scribble 12		Zigzag or waving line
Scribble 13		Single loop line
Scribble 14		Multiple loop line
Scribble 15		Spiral line
Scribble 16		Multiple-line overlaid circle
Scribble 17		Multiple-line circumference circle
Scribble 18		Circular line spread out
Scribble 19		Single crossed circle
Scribble 20		Imperfect circle

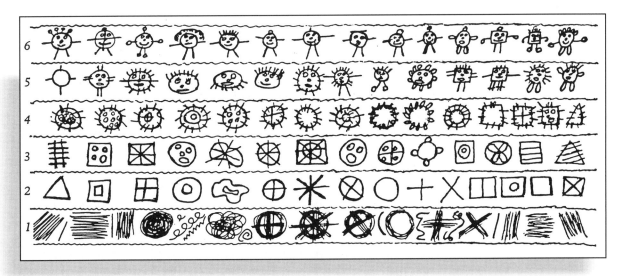

'loopy' or included whirls and, on the other, those which involved repeated parallel lines. It seems to me that Claire Golomb and Linda Whitaker identified the two particular kinds of scribble described all those years ago by D.R. Major (1906) (*see Figure 1*).

In my own research I have found that after their earlier more exuberant scribbles *some* children may produce carefully controlled shapes and patterns along the lines described by Rhoda Kellogg, and this seems to indicate that they are gaining more skill at manipulating the pencil and are interested in experimenting with different shapes. But not all children necessarily do this; some simply go on filling the page with 'sheer scribble'. So, it is not essential for children to produce the more carefully drawn shapes before they move on to representational drawing. In fact, although we tend to think of scribbling as a necessary early step in drawing there is no solid evidence that there would be a problem if children missed this experience altogether. And, indeed, there are examples of children in our own society and in others who have not had the opportunity to draw but later, when provided with pencil and paper, have produced recognizable figures often within the first half hour of experimenting with paper and pencil. This important observation was made by an anthropologist, Alexander Alland (1983), who visited a number of different cultures. What is particularly interesting is that the children's first encounters with the drawing materials were filmed so that there is a true record of their reactions and the actual process of drawing as well as the finished products. Alexander Alland found that there was not much evidence that the 'milestones' of early drawing development followed by western children occurred at similar ages in these other societies. Children did not necessarily draw the circles or mandalas claimed by Rhoda Kellogg to be universal. In fact, Alland came to the conclusion that the idea of a universal pattern of development in drawing has been much exaggerated.

Rhoda Kellogg believed that all children have an innate, aesthetic sense and that their scribbles reflect an urge to construct balanced, pleasing shapes; she claimed that children are not concerned with representing real objects, so their scribbles don't 'stand for' things in the real world. In fact, this is another aspect of her work which has been challenged. John Matthews (1984) has shown that children's scribbles sometimes *are* representational even if we adults don't recognize anything in them. He gives an example of Ben, aged 2 years 1 month, who made a series of overlapping loops on the page (*see Plate 1, p. viii*) and, while he was doing this, excitedly gave a running commentary: '...it's going round the corner. It's going round the corner. It's gone now'. Ben was probably describing the movement of an imaginary car going round the corner until it disappeared out of sight. So, Ben's scribble was not representational in the sense that it *looked* like a car; what he captured was the action or movement of the car. But this is representational; it has meaning and relates to something in the real world. It's not surprising, then, that John Matthews calls this sort of thing an 'action representation'. We should be careful, however, not to get carried away and imagine that all scribbles are action representations. Often, when I asked my 2-year-old daughter about her pictures she would say, 'I'm just scribbling'.

It's not clear from John Matthews' example whether Ben intended the car, or rather its movement, to be the subject of his picture *before* he began or whether he had already begun a spontaneous movement that then perhaps reminded him of a car. Sometimes when children are scribbling or experimenting with shapes they 'see things' in their pictures. For example, my daughter, at 2 years 10 months, drew a closed shape and said, 'Look! That's a bird'. Then she said, 'He needs an eye' and added a dot in the appropriate place. Then she gave it some legs, 'They have legs, don't they? Five legs!' (*see Figure 4*). The French researcher Georges-Henri Luquet (1913) also noticed that his daughter Simonne sometimes saw things in her scribbles and he used the term 'fortuitous realism' to describe the child's accidental discovery. At this stage, however, children may not be able to hang on to the idea of what they want to draw even if they accidentally discover a particular shape in their scribbles. D.R. Major (1906) noticed that his son frequently changed his mind as to the thing he wanted to draw when the lines seemed to suggest a new object.

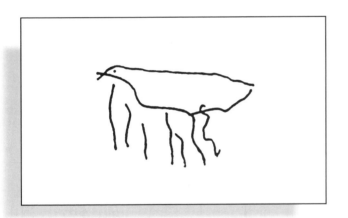

Figure 4: Amy, aged 2 years 10 months, decided she had drawn a bird shape. She added an eye and some legs.

So far, I have been talking about children's spontaneous drawings, those that they do for themselves. What if we ask these children, who are still at the scribbling stage, to draw a figure especially for us? In this case, *we* decide the subject for them before they begin, so we give them an intention. Let's say that we ask them to draw 'a man' or 'a lady'. A few children will refuse, saying simply, 'I can't' or 'I don't know how to draw a man'. Having said that he didn't know 'how to do a man' a little boy in Amelia Fysh's nursery was asked to try. At first he replied, 'I don't know how to try' but then managed to do a few scribbles (*see Figure 52*). Indeed, most children will draw something. Although some will produce a long wavy scribble (*see Figure 10*) or a more exuberant scribble all over the page (*see Figures 25, 34, 37 and 39*), many children will produce a more 'contained' scribble or shape which may represent

8

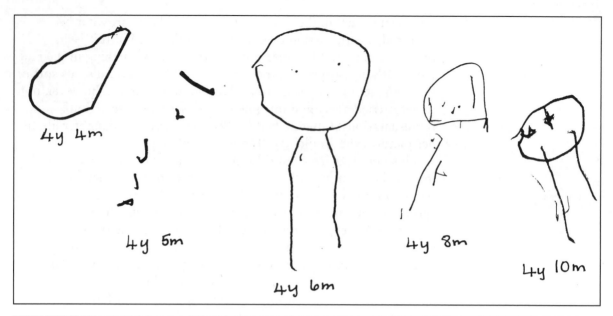

4y 4m

4y 5m

4y 6m

4y 8m

4y 10m

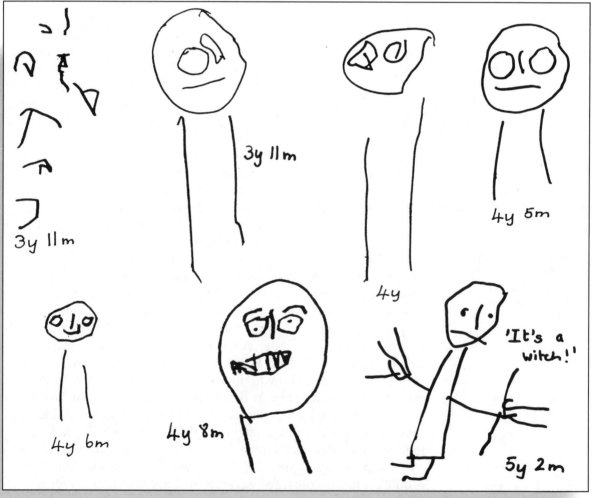

3y 11m

3y 11m

4y 6m

4y 8m

4y

4y 5m

'It's a witch!!'

5y 2m

Figure 5: *(top left)* This boy's first drawing stands for a whole person. In the second, each mark indicates different parts of the figure. (AF5a)

Figure 6: *(bottom left)* This boy's first attempt at a figure is a series of marks. The face of this tadpole figure gradually becomes more elaborate. (AF5b)

Figure 7: *(below)* Some of the elements of a human figure are present in Helen's early attempts and are roughly in the correct places. (AF45)

the whole figure (*see Figures 5, 22 and 40*) or a series of smaller shapes or lines which may indicate different parts of a person (*see Figures 5, 6, 28, 32 and 42*). When Claire Golomb and Linda Whitaker (Golomb, 1981) asked their scribblers to draw a person 40 per cent of the 2-year-olds and 80 per cent of the 3-year-olds produced much more carefully contoured forms than their usual scribbles.

Sometimes in response to the request to draw a person children produce scribbles that we would not immediately recognize as a human figure, but if we look at them in the context of the child's later figures we can see the early emergence of certain elements that are used in these later figures. These elements may be disconnected but they may still be in rough spatial correspondence to the main body parts of a real person. (*See Figures 7, 8 and 15.*)

Although these children cannot draw a figure that we easily recognize as a human form they can often express quite a lot of what they know if we give them a bit of help. For example, if we

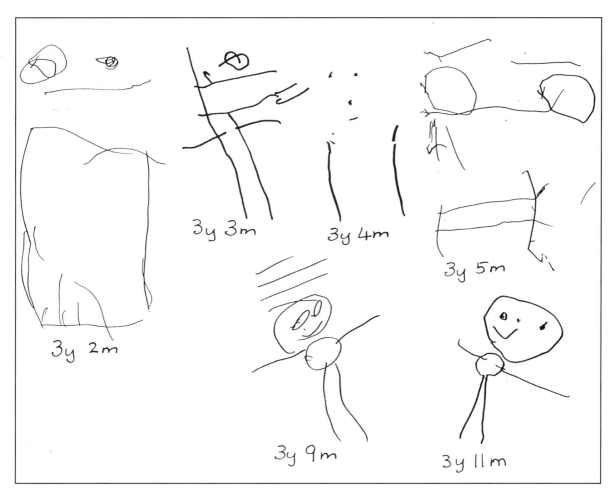

3y 3m

3y 4m

3y 5m

3y 2m

3y 9m

3y 11m

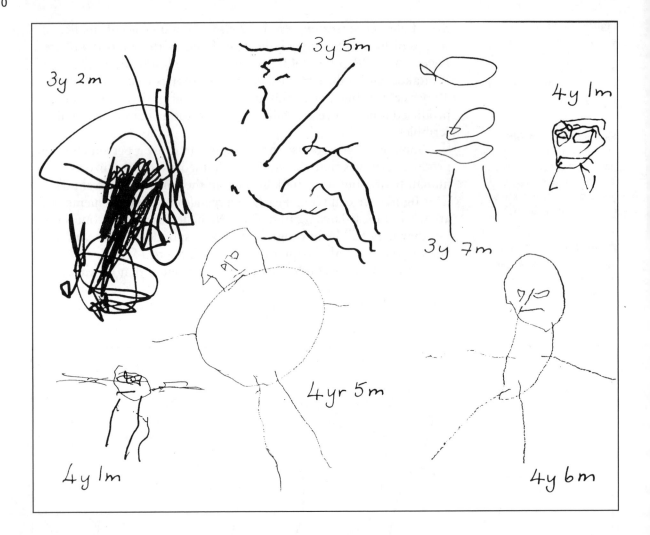

3y 2m

3y 5m

4y 1m

3y 7m

4y 5m

4y 1m

4y 6m

Figure 8: After two early scribbles Peter, aged 3 years 7 months, begins to work out the basic elements of a human figure. (AF98)

begin to sketch a human figure – starting with the head and a body – scribblers may then be able to add the arms and the legs and, perhaps, a number of other details as well (*see Figure 73*). So, these children may not know how to *start* a drawing but once having started – either by accidentally spotting something in their own scribbles or having an adult start them off – they can add the finishing touches.

2

Tadpole figures

So, what are children's first recognizable human figures like? It is well known in the research literature on children's drawings that the first figures are very rudimentary, usually consisting of a roughly circular, closed shape with two straight lines protruding down vertically from the bottom of it. Often this is all (*see Figure 9*). These early figures are called 'tadpole figures' or simply 'tadpoles' because they seem to be 'all head' and the legs look a bit like a tadpole's 'tail'. But some children's figures are more elaborate, with facial features added, most commonly eyes and perhaps a mouth, but less frequently a nose. Sometimes the arms are drawn but they will probably be attached to the sides of the head. Some figures may have additional features such as hair, feet, hands, and so on. (*See Figures 5, 6, 19, 20, 22 and many others throughout this book.*)

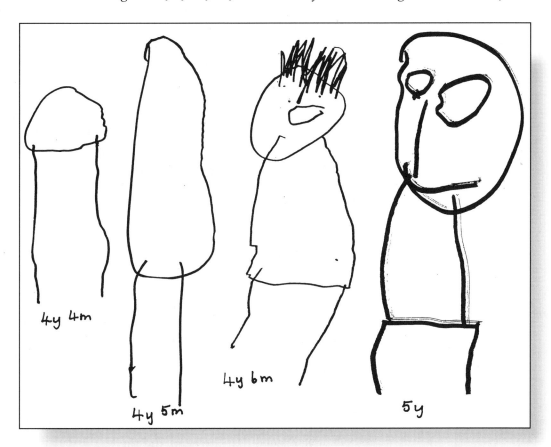

4y 4m

4y 5m

4y 6m

5y

Figure 9: Martin's tadpole figure, drawn at 4 years 4 months, has no facial features. Later, a body is created by adding a horizontal line and then extra legs beneath. (AF150)

Perhaps the most striking thing about the tadpole figure is the omission of the torso. Is it likely that the figure really is bodiless? Some writers, such as Rudolf Arnheim (1974), have argued that the body has already been included; he suggested that the 'head' is not only a head but a combined head and torso, a sort of Mr Man figure. If this were so then the position of the arms would not be so peculiar after all. Well, if it were true that the tadpole figure has a body then we might expect children to mention this fact if questioned about their figures. Some of my students asked 100 tadpole-drawers to identify each part of their figures. Only one child had drawn anything which we normally associate with the torso: she had drawn a 'tummy-button' inside the head circle of her figure. None of the other 99 children mentioned a body or anything to do with the torso; the head circle was simply described as a 'head', and nothing more. So, although a child may very occasionally draw a tummy or a tummy-button inside the head circle we think it very unlikely that the head circle is normally meant to include the torso.

But why should children draw only a head and legs, with perhaps some arms and a few other details added? Why is the torso missed out? It seems to us adults to be a very large and fundamental part of the human form. Pre-school children certainly *know* about bodies and tummies and they also know that arms don't stick out of people's heads. It is not that they are ignorant; neither is there any evidence that they imagine real people to look like the ones in their pictures. The problem is to do with the actual process of drawing. Producing a drawing is not like taking a photograph of an object where there is a direct transfer of the image onto the film; it is a much more complicated affair. The child has to decide which parts of a person to draw, how to draw each part, where to put each part in relation to each other part, how to fix the parts together, and so on. And there can be problems with any of these components of the task.

To start with, let's consider the issue of which parts a child might choose to include in the figure. Although she has seen lots of pictures of people and she has no doubt also witnessed teachers, parents and other children actually in the process of drawing she probably hasn't been shown exactly, step by step, how they do it. So, she only has a hazy idea of how to go about the task. What people normally draw first is the head and, indeed, the head may be the most important and defining thing about the human figure, so it is not surprising that that is where the child usually begins. But what next? She probably cannot remember what other people do. If she tries to imagine what the human figure is like she may latch on to the idea that it is an upright creature on two long legs. Certainly a number of researchers (e.g., Kerschensteiner, 1905; Luquet, 1913; Golomb, 1981) have argued that the head and the legs are its two most defining features. The young child is also limited in the extent to which she can recall or 'capture' in her mind the features of the figure in her drawing; given this limitation it is likely to be the most defining features that she is able to think of.

Of course, it would be very difficult if not impossible simply to add a torso to the tadpole figure; once the legs have been drawn there is nowhere for it to go. Furthermore, since the tadpole-drawers haven't had cause to draw the torso they may not know how to draw it. If questioned, some children will say, 'My lady doesn't have a body', or simply, 'I can't draw bodies'. My students and I have carried out a series of studies with tadpole-drawers and have found that they become very attached to their tadpole figure formula and are very reluctant to leave it behind (see Cox, 1992 and 1993). In one study we asked twenty-two tadpole-drawers to watch while we drew a conventional figure (a head and facial features, a body, arms and legs); we named each body part as it was being drawn. We called this group the 'whole figure' group. When the children were asked to copy the figure, twelve of them (55 per cent) drew a reasonably accurate conventional figure. Another group of twenty-two tadpole-drawers was also asked to watch while we drew a conventional figure but this group copied each body part immediately after we had drawn it. We called them the 'segment' group. Fifteen children (68 per cent) produced a conventional figure. We had yet another group of eighteen children (the 'repeated segment' group) who had the same treatment as the segment group but copied three figures in all. By the third figure thirteen of them (72 per cent) drew conventional forms. We also asked some 'control' children simply to repeat the drawing task and these children carried on drawing their usual tadpole form, confirming our hunch that the tadpole form is well entrenched and tadpole-drawers cannot easily be persuaded to relinquish it.

We were keen to find out whether those children who had been able or willing to copy the conventional figure would adopt this new structure. So, we went back two days later and asked all the children to draw a person for us. Most of the children in the 'whole figure' and the 'segment' groups produced a tadpole form; only five children in each group (23 per cent) drew a conventional figure. Only in the 'repeated segment' group did the majority of the children (61 per cent) draw a conventional figure.

When they draw their first tadpole figure children are usually delighted to have produced something even vaguely recognizable and teachers and parents will praise their success. Adults rarely criticize these early efforts. Having found a way of drawing a figure a child may produce this 'formula' on subsequent occasions. In other words, the formula becomes practised and fairly automatic; the child doesn't have to work it out afresh every time. She 'knows how to draw people'. (*See Figures 6, 10, 20, 21 and 22.*) This doesn't mean that the figure looks *exactly* the same every time. In fact, as she gets more practised the child may add extra parts such as hair, arms or feet of her own accord or at the suggestion of other children or adults. But, for very many children, the basic structure of the figure remains for some time with, most notably, the torso missed out.

3y 5m

3y 10m

3y 11m

4y 2m

4y 3m

4y 4m

4y 6m

4y 7m

4y 7m

4y 8m

4y 8m

5y 1m

Figure 10: *(left)* Andrian's unusual style of figure persisted for several months. The final figure in the set was drawn at infants school. (AF79)

Figure 11: This boy, aged 4 years 2 months, drew a transitional figure; 6 months later he drew a tadpole form after watching another child draw but also spontaneously drew quite a skilful conventional figure. (AF241)

Some people have assumed that children copy their tadpole forms either from other children or from the Mr Men characters in books, television cartoons and on yoghurt pots. We know that a few children do copy directly from other sources. For example, Amelia Fysh noted that the tadpole form in Figure 11 was drawn by a boy, aged 4 years 8 months, after he had watched another child draw a figure. Shortly after this he produced a very elaborate conventional figure. And, in fact, over six months previously he had drawn a figure 'transitional' between a tadpole and a conventional form. But there is no evidence that most children routinely copy directly from others and every possibility that they have worked out how to draw the tadpole form on their own. There are a number of examples of tadpole-drawers who were eldest or 'only' children and who also did not go to nursery or mix with other children; they could not have seen other children drawing tadpole figures. The Norwegian psychologist, Helga Eng, carried out a longitudinal study of her niece Margaret and noted that Margaret's discovery of the tadpole form was made on her own and not influenced by other children's work (Eng, 1931).

Historically, children have been drawing tadpole figures for as long as children's drawings have been a serious topic of study. A short pamphlet on children's drawings published in 1887 by Corrado Ricci included some tadpole figures drawn by Italian children in 1885 (*see Figure 12*), a very long time before the Mr Men books were written!

Figure 12: Tadpole figures drawn by an Italian child in 1885.

Figure 13: *(top right)* A pre-drawn figure of a man was available for 'R' to copy (nos. 1–6). No. 7 was drawn from memory.

Figure 15: *(bottom right)* There is no head contour around the facial features of this child's early figures. (AF259)

In 1906 D.R. Major reported his attempts over several months to persuade his son to copy a man drawn for him (*see Figure 13*). Some progress was made from the first disconnected scrawls at age 2 years and 4 months to the more complex patterns of lines and closed shapes produced a few months later; in general, though, R's attempts did not look much like the model. The week after his third birthday R drew a tadpole figure from imagination; there was no obvious torso although he said that a line dangling down from one arm was a 'dress'. So, even when children have had the model of a conventional figure available to them, and in this case have been encouraged to copy it over a period of months, they may still produce the tadpole form. My observations in the nursery school also lead me to conclude that tadpole-drawers do not pay much close attention to other children's drawings and do not routinely use them as their models; they seem to be intent on solving the problem of how to draw for themselves. The fact that very young children may not closely scrutinize other drawings does not of course mean that they are not influenced by them at all. The conventional figures that they see around them may provide a *general idea* of what they might aspire to even if they do not attempt to copy the exact way they are produced.

Although most children draw a circle, or a roughly circular shape, for the head of their figures there are some exceptions. Occasionally a child draws the facial features without an enclosing circle and then simply adds some legs below (*see Figures 7, 14 and 15*). There are also cases where the head contour is drawn as an arch, not joined at the bottom (*see Figure 16*), or it may be like a square with the lower line missing (*see Figure 10*).

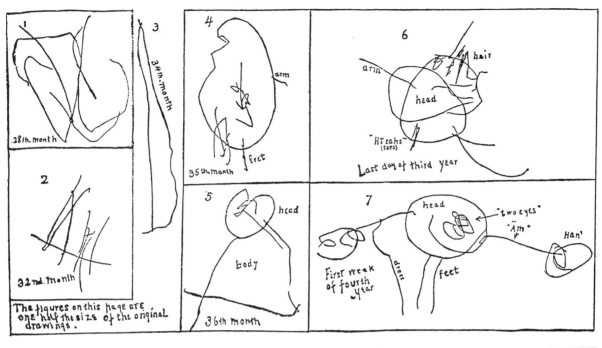

Within the figure panels:

1 — 28th. month
3 — 34th. month
2 — 32nd. Month
The figures on this page are one half the size of the original drawings.
4 — arm — feet — 35th. month
5 — head — body — 36th month
6 — arin — hair — head — "Hteahs" (ears) — Last day of third year
7 — head — "two eyes" — "Am" — Han' — dress — feet — First week of fourth year

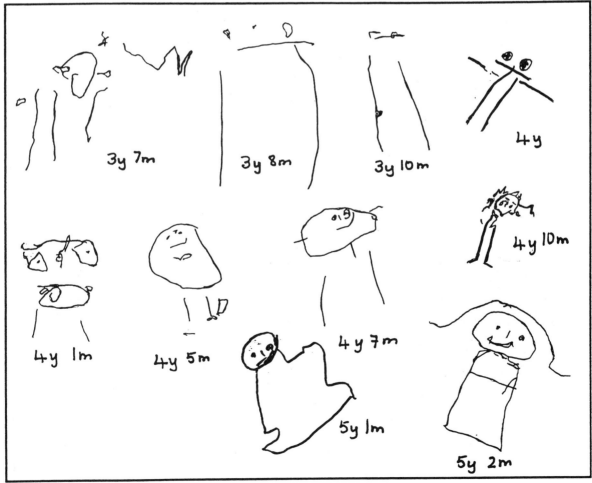

3y 7m

3y 8m

3y 10m

4y

4y 1m

4y 5m

4y 7m

4y 10m

5y 1m

5y 2m

3y 10m

3y 10m

3y 11m

4y

4y 3m

4y 5m

4y 8m

4y 11m

5y 2m

Figure 14: *(left)* Linda's early figures have facial features but no head contour.(AF65a)

Figure 16: *(right)* The head contour of this boy's early figures is incomplete. (AF203)

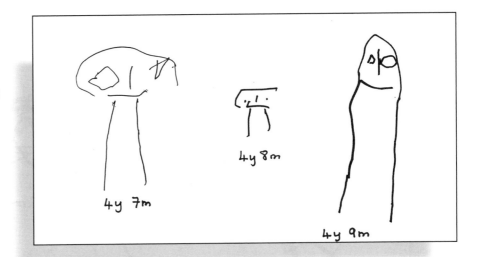

Some children do not draw their figures the 'right way up', but draw them sideways (*see Figure 39*), on a slant or even upside-down (*see Figure 17*). The reason is not always clear. It may be that young children have not yet learned the conventions of drawing on a flat piece of paper; they may not know that the part nearest to them is the ground and the part furthest from them is 'up in the air'. But it may also be that sometimes the child has accidentally drawn the head of the figure too close to the bottom of the page. One way out of this difficulty is to draw the figure upside-down and then,

Figure 17: *(right)* Claire, aged 4 years 2 months, has drawn the members of her family in different orientations on the page.

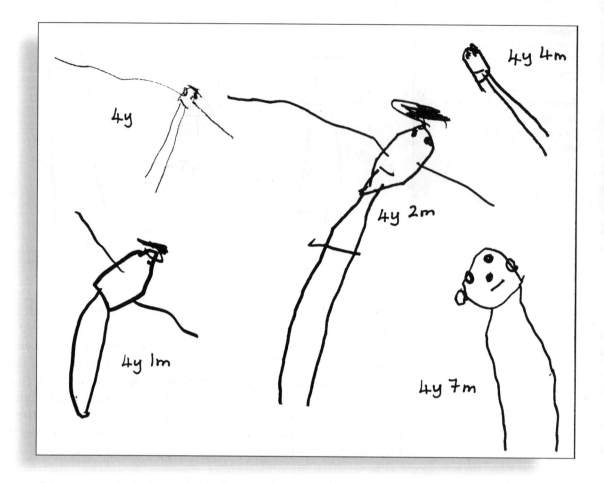

4y

4y 4m

4y 2m

4y 1m

4y 7m

Figure 18: A 4-year-old girl's slanted figures. (AF40a)

perhaps, to turn the page round. Another possible reason for non-upright figures is that, again by accident, the child may have placed the eyes of the figure too low down in the head or on a slant. This 'error' then determines the positioning of the rest of the figure. (*See Figures 18 and 25*.)

Children vary in the period of time over which they draw tadpole figures. Some have a very short phase; for example, my daughter drew only three tadpole figures, each on three consecutive days. Others, however, carry on drawing tadpole figures over a period of weeks or even months (*see Figure 19*). There is no reason to believe that children who retain the tadpole form for longer are any less intellectually able than those who dispense with it early, except in exceptional cases where the tadpole figure is retained well into the infants school years, and even then there may be other reasons why this occurs.

Even within a small sample of tadpole figures we can sometimes see development taking place. Usually the most obvious change is a shift from the rather diffident use of line in the earlier figures to an assured use of line and shape later on. Some children start to add

Figure 19: Tony drew tadpole figures over a period of several months. At age 5 years 5 months in the infants school he draws legs with double lines and also includes the feet with this contour. He also adds ears. (AF86)

extra items to their figures: in Figure 20 only the eyes are included in the earlier faces but a nose and mouth have been added to later ones; similarly, the earlier tadpole figures have scribbled hair whereas the hair in the last two tadpoles has a more definite spiky shape. Many children, however, do seem to have a set formula for their tadpole figure and they alter it hardly at all until eventually they produce a more conventional figure (*see Figures 21 and 22*).

There are some children who miss out the tadpole stage and go straight on to drawing a conventional figure which includes a body, and the arms are located on the body and not the head. In these cases parents, brothers and sisters or friends may have taught the child how to draw the figure. There are also some children who have not received specific tuition but have managed to copy someone else's drawing of a conventional figure. On the whole, though, there are rather few of these cases and most children draw

3y 11m

4y 1m

4y 2m

4y 3m

4y 5m

4y 7m

4y 11m

5y 1m

5y 1m

Figure 20: *(above)* Simon's first tadpole figures have eyes and scribbled hair. Later, he adds a nose and a mouth and makes the hair more stylish. (AF54)

Figure 21: *(top right)* Joanna uses a similar formula for all her tadpole figures before she draws a more conventional form at age 4 years 8 months. When she goes to infants school she draws a tadpole figure again. (AF40b)

Figure 22: *(bottom right)* Teresa's tadpole figures have similar features. (AF43)

tadpole figures even if only for a brief period of time. As a researcher it is difficult to be sure that a child has definitely missed out a tadpole stage since it is always possible that he drew a tadpole figure at home or at nursery but that it simply went unnoticed or unrecorded.

4y

4y 1m

4y 4m

4y 8 m

4y 8m

5y 1m

4y 1m

4y 3m

4y 6m

4y 7m

4y 9m

3

The transitional

figure

It has been known for a long time (Luquet, 1920; Gridley, 1938; Arnheim, 1974) that some young children draw a version of the human figure which is a bit like a tadpole figure in that it doesn't have an enclosed body, but the arms are attached to the legs (rather than the head) and any 'body' features such as the belly-button, buttons or clothing are placed in the space between the legs and where the body 'ought to be'. Rudolf Arnheim (1974) gives an example of a child's drawing showing a house in the centre with two fish in it (*see Figure 23*). To the right is a cowboy and to the left is a cow. Note that both figures have a similar structure: the arms are placed on the vertical 'legs', which Arnheim asserts are an undifferentiated representation of the torso and the legs, and the cowboy's stomach and the cow's two stomachs are located in the body space. Incidentally, it is also interesting to note that young children often use the same formula for drawing humans and animals (*see Figures 23 and 38*).

The children who draw these transitional figures tend to be a little older than the tadpole-drawers but younger than those who draw a definite enclosed unit for the body, and it is for this reason that I call these figures 'transitional'. In a study of forty-two pre-school children, Charmian Parkin and I (Cox and Parkin, 1986) found that those who drew tadpole forms were aged from 2 years 11 months to 3 years 5 months (the average age was 3 years) and those who drew transitional forms were aged from 3 years to 4 years 5 months (with an average age of 3 years 8 months); the youngest child in the nursery at that time to draw a conventional figure was aged 3 years 10 months.

Although many children progress from drawing a tadpole figure to the transitional and then on to the conventional form (*see Figure 24*) not all children follow this pattern; many miss out the transitional figure altogether (*see Figures 8, 9, 21, 22 and 25*). On the other hand, there are fewer who have missed out the tadpole 'stage' and have progressed from scribbling directly to a transitional figure or to a conventional form.

Figure 23: *(right)* Two fish inside a house (centre), a cowboy with one stomach (right) and a cow with two stomachs (left).

Figure 24: *(bottom)* After drawing a scribbled shape Helen progresses through tadpole and transitional forms to a conventional figure. (AF64)

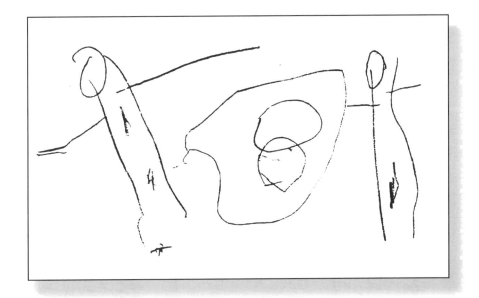

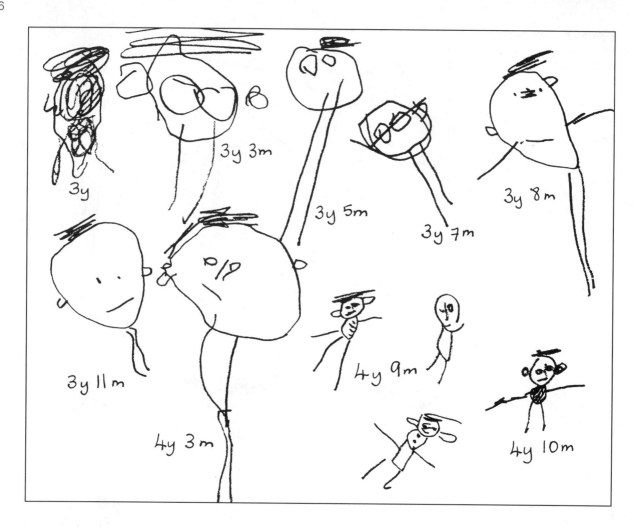

Figure 25: Helen progresses from tadpole forms to conventional figures at age 4 years 3 months. (AF90)

4

Drawing the
body

Some years ago Jacqueline Goodnow (1977) claimed that children produce a conventional figure by adapting their tadpole or transitional figures and that they do this simply by adding a cross-line between the legs (*see Figure 26*). This sounds like a very easy and straightforward change for the child to make. What evidence is there that this is what children actually do? In Amelia Fysh's collection only 4 per cent of the children clearly drew a cross-line on a tadpole or transitional form. About half the children however did turn the legs of these early figures into a body but in slightly different ways from that suggested by Jacqueline Goodnow. Some seemed to do it by drawing two vertical lines down from the head and joining them with a horizontal line at the bottom; then they added two legs underneath. Others drew one vertical line down from the head and then, without lifting the pencil, sharply changed direction and drew the horizontal line; the second vertical line of the body was drawn next and then the legs were added. In all these cases the body has a very 'angular' appearance. (*See Figures 27 and 28.*)

Figure 26: *(right)* Turning a tadpole figure (a) into a conventional figure (b) by adding a cross-line between the legs.

Figure 28: *(bottom)* Mark progresses from scribbles to tadpole forms to conventional figures at age 4 years. (AF126)

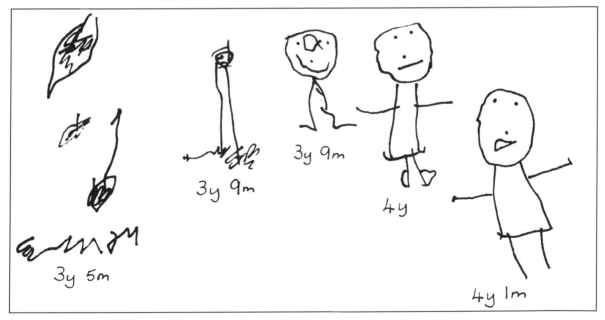

3y 10m

3y 11m

3y 11m

4y 1m

4y 2m

4y 2m

Figure 27: *(above)* Alan constructs the body of his conventional figures with two verticals closed at the bottom with a horizontal line; the legs are drawn underneath. (AF159)

Figure 29: *(top right)* Jan draws separate circles for the head and body of her first three conventional figures. In the last one, she has looped the body line down from the head and back up again. (AF149)

Figure 30: *(bottom right)* Glen draws the body of his conventional figures by appending a loop below the head circle. At age 4 years 5 months he tries some 'loopy' arms. (AF148)

The other half of the sample drew a more rounded body. A few children drew a separate circle or oval for the body and placed it immediately below the head (*see Figure 29*) and sometimes the two contours markedly overlap (*see Figure 39*). But most children started a line from the head and then looped it down and back up again, so that the body is appended to the head (*see Figures 30, 34 and 36*).

Occasionally there are some children who do not fit any of these patterns. For example, one child drew stick men (*see Figure 31*). Of course, it may be that she developed it for herself. On the other hand, stick figures are actually rather rare and in this case the figures are drawn very confidently from the beginning as if the child had been shown how to construct them and had probably practised them at home. Incidentally, it seems to be an adult fantasy that the stick figure is a typically childish way of drawing and adults are often surprised to find how rarely children actually produce it. Another less frequent form is the outline figure in which the whole or a large part is drawn with a continuous line, so that the final

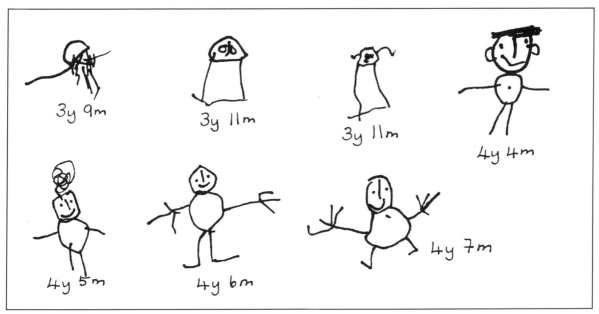

Figure 31: *(bottom)* Susan is unusual in drawing 'stick' figures; most children draw an enclosed contour for the body. (AF25)

Figure 32: *(right)* Karen experiments with a continuous outline. (AF11)

Figure 33: *(page 31)* As soon as he starts to draw conventional figures at the age of 4 years 6 months Jan experiments with body shape. He dashes off eight portraits within 5 minutes. (AF23)

figure looks a bit like a gingerbread man (*see Figures 15 and 32*); this is also called 'threading'. A further exception in the sample is a figure which has a neck and an 'upside-down' triangular body (*see Figure 33, lower left*). Jan, the boy who drew this figure, handled the pencil extremely confidently and his subsequent figures show an interest in experimenting with different body shapes and other features of the figures.

3y 7m

4y 2m

4y 2m

4y 6m

4y 6m

4y 10m

4y 11m

4y 11m

Mrs Fysh

Mrs Hancock

Mrs Pinder

Mrs Hasted

Miss Howarth

Mrs Cornell

Mrs Wyatt

Mrs Whyte

5

Is there an

orderly

development?

Figure 34: (right) Over a 2-month period Julie progresses from scribbles, to tadpole figures to a conventional form. (AF106)

Figure 35: (page 34) Valerie draws her first conventional figure before the summer holiday but in September she reverts to a tadpole form. The triangular skirts and the hairstyles and bows indicate the gender of the figures. (AF32c)

Figure 36: (page 35, top) Martin begins to draw conventional figures at age 4 years but draws a tadpole form at age 4 years 3 months after a summer holiday. (AF49a)

Figure 37: (page 35, bottom) Amongst her conventional figures Rachel drew two tadpole forms at age 3 years 10 months and 3 years 11 months and a transitional form at 4 years 2 months. (AF164)

So far I have presented rather an orderly progression of development from scribbling or simple shapes, to tadpole figures, to transitional figures (for some but not all children) and then to conventional figures. There are indeed many children who fit this orderly pattern (*see Figures 24, 25, 28 and 34*). There are others for whom the pattern is broadly true but not quite so clear-cut, and others for whom it is very messy. For those children whose progression is very orderly they seem to move from one distinct 'stage' to the next. While in the tadpole stage, for example, all their figures are tadpoles; then they draw only transitional figures and finally only conventional figures. Each stage seems to be 'of a piece' and a step forwards towards producing more and more mature figures.

Many children, however, will 'lapse' into scribbling even though they have already produced a tadpole figure. After my daughter drew three tadpole figures she was only interested in scribbling for seven or eight weeks before eventually drawing a conventional figure. Even when she had practised and developed her conventional figures she often took pleasure simply in scribbling. This is not at all unusual. Children often go through these phases and especially in the summertime they may lose interest in drawing altogether but pick it up again in the autumn with renewed interest.

As well as the periodic lapses into scribbling many children also show an unevenness in their progress with their human figure drawing. For example, Valerie (*see Figure 35*) drew a conventional figure but then lapsed back into drawing a tadpole figure before eventually drawing conventional forms again. (*Other examples can be found in Figures 36 and 37.*) A little girl called Joanna drew tadpole figures and then conventional figures in the nursery school but when she moved to the infants school she drew a tadpole figure again (*see Figure 21*). A number of children seem to display this temporary 'lapse', particularly after a holiday when they may not have practised their drawing.

One little boy called Aidan that Charmian Parkin and I studied (Cox and Parkin, 1986) mixed tadpole figures, transitional forms and conventional figures over a period of months before he eventually drew only conventional figures. There is a lovely example provided by Helga Eng (1931) of all three forms drawn on the same page (*see Figure 38*): her niece Margaret drew a bear (a tadpole figure), a monkey (a conventional figure) and a man (a transitional figure). (*Also, see Figure 64.*) It is not known why some children progress in a more stage-like way and others have a more mixed development. With very few exceptions, though, all of them will develop a conventional figure, use it consistently and go on to develop it further. The often uneven progress is summed up by Joseph Di Leo (1970): 'Viewed in perspective, the development of

4y 6m

4y 8m

4y 8m

4y 9m

4y 10m

4y 10m

My family
9 yrs.

3y 8m

3y 10m

4y 1m

4y 3m

4y 5m

4y 7m

4y 7m

4y 7m

4y 10m

4y 11m

5y 4m

'My family'

9 yrs.

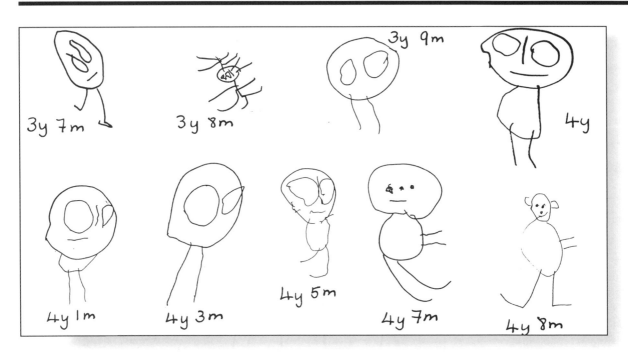

behavior advances towards maturity, but its course is not straight and even. In every field of behavior there are forward thrusts, backward slides, pauses, and renewed thrusts. Only the broad view will reveal the advance' (p. 96).

Figure 38: A bear, a monkey and a person (from left to right) – three different forms drawn in the same scene.

6

Is development universal?

I mentioned earlier that, on the whole, very young children do not routinely appear to copy directly from other children or other sources. Does this mean, then, that all children everywhere start off by representing the human figure in the same way? In other words, is the development through scribbling to the tadpole figure and then later to a more conventional figure universal? In order to answer this question we would have to investigate children's drawings in a society which has not been influenced by western images. With the spread of western culture this is almost impossible these days. However, there are still cultures in which the indigenous art forms are different from those in the West and also remain strong. One example is the Warlpiri group of Aboriginal peoples in Australia.

The Warlpiri use a horse-shoe shape to represent a person and the children frequently see this shape when adults illustrate their stories by drawing in the sand; adult artists also use the shape in their paintings on canvas or bark, or in their ceremonial body painting. The children use this shape when they themselves start to draw but they also see and use western forms of depiction at the community's school. To date, there has been no detailed investigation of these children's work but I have examined a small collection of their pictures gathered by Rosemary Hill when she visited the community at Yuendumu to produce a BBC/Open University television programme on children's drawings. Sometimes the children use only Warlpiri images; sometimes they use both Warlpiri and western ones and may mix them in the same picture. Roseanne who is 6 years old draws a simple curved line to stand for a person (*see Plate 2a*) whereas Kylie (*see Plate 2b*) and Stephanie (*see Plate 2c*), who are 8, produce enclosed forms, more like the adult 'horse-shoe' symbols. Roseanne's western-style person is a tadpole figure whereas the babies in Stephanie's picture are conventional figures.

Plate 2a Roseanne, aged 6 years, has drawn tadpole figures and the Warlpiri symbol for a person in the same picture.

Plate 2b Kylie, aged 8 years, has used exclusively Warlpiri symbols in her picture. The curved shapes are women – each has a baby-carrier and a planting stick – who are telling a story about a journey to a well.

Plate 2c Stephanie, aged 8 years, uses the Warlpiri symbol to depict groups of people around their camp-fires. The babies in their carriers are drawn in a western style.

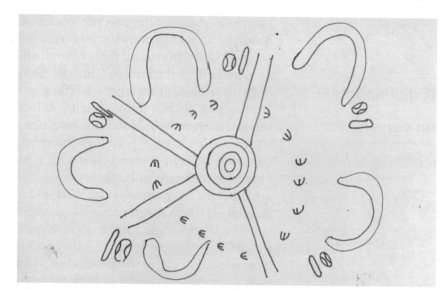

These pictures suggest, then, that children will pick up ways of drawing from their surrounding culture even if they have not been taught to copy them in any direct way. Furthermore, their attempts to produce a particular image will go through a certain amount of development – from a simple curve to an enclosed curved space in the Warlpiri tradition or a tadpole form to a conventional figure in the western style of depiction. It appears that the children's earlier attempts in both systems are their own approximations to the particular cultural forms they are aspiring to. (See Cox, 1993, for a more extended discussion of cultural influences on children's drawing.)

7

Adapting the

conventional

figure

As children grow older in westernized cultures they add more features to their figures. As well as the head contour, legs and eyes the main extra items are the torso, the arms, the mouth and nose, hair, hands and feet. But it is not particularly unusual for the arms, hands, feet and nose to be omitted. The ears and neck are fairly uncommon in the figure drawings of even 5- to 6-year-olds. Although the heads, hands and feet of their figures may be disproportionately large the figures generally look as if all their parts are located in more or less the appropriate places; if the arms are included they are almost always attached to the torso and not to the head.

Some children start off by drawing the torso of their figures in a more rounded way whereas others construct them as more angular forms. In the short term they may draw the bodies of all their figures in a similar way (*see Figure 39*), but many children experiment with the shape of the torso, making it more rounded, more square or more triangular, and a few try out a continuous outline or 'threading' for the torso and other adjoining body parts (*see Figures 40, 41 and 50*). After drawing a couple of figures on the same page Jan volunteered to do some more and completed eight in less than 5 minutes (*see Figure 33*).

Figure 39: *(page 40)* Daren's figures at age 4 years 9 months are all constructed in the same way. (AF10)

Figure 40: *(right)* This 4-year-old girl uses a continuous outline or 'threading' in her conventional figures. (AF28a)

Figure 41: *(page 41)* Angeli's early figures have rounded bodies; at 4 years 2 months she experiments with a continuous outline. The long hair (even in the early figures) and clothing denote the female gender. (AF3)

Since arms and legs are long things it is not surprising that nearly all young children almost invariably use single lines or 'sticks' to represent them. The main alternative is to use double lines so that the limbs look more like 'tubes'. When I examined a sample of seventy-four tadpole and transitional figures (Cox, 1993) 84 per cent of those which had arms were drawn with single lines and 96 per cent of those which had legs were drawn with single lines; only a very small minority had tubular limbs. When children introduce a body to their figures they may still draw stick-like arms and legs. But, increasingly, they change to a tubular form. In Amelia Fysh's

4y 4m

A lady

A man

Man

Lady

4y 6m

man

Lady

4y 8m

4y 8m

4y 8m

A baby
4y 9m

Daddy

4y 9m

Mummy

4y 9m

Aunty Sue

5y

5y 2m

3y 2m

3y 3m

3y 4m

3y 5m

3y 6m

3y 7m

3y 8m

3y 9m

3y 10m

3y 11m

4y 2m

4y 6m

4y 7m

4y 8m

4y 11m

5y

Figure 42: *(right)* Lee changes from single to double lines to depict the arms and legs of her figures. (AF161)

collection approximately 60 per cent of the children were drawing stick-like limbs when they left the nursery and 40 per cent were either drawing tubular limbs routinely or had begun to experiment with them (*see Figure 42*). By the age of about 6 years most children have adopted the tubular form for the limbs of their figures. Most children add the 'tube' to the body with two lines and then either close it off with a line or add a hand or foot on the end (*see Figures 35 and 42*). Others draw a more 'loopy' limb which may sometimes outline the fingers too (*see Figures 30, 41 and 43*). One or two make the limb thicker simply by repeatedly going backwards and forwards over it with the pencil (*see Figure 44*). A few children draw the arms and the body as one contoured unit (*see Figures 32, 41 and 50*); one or two do a similar thing with the lower torso and the legs (*see Figures 40 and 45*).

3y 8m

3y 11m

4 y

4y 6m

4y 5m

4y 8m

4y 8m

4y 10m

4y 10m

44

3y 2m

3y 6m

3y 10m

3y 10m

4y
A girl
with her
Mummy

4y 3m

Me

Mrs Fysh

Mummy

Mrs Fysh

Mummy

Me

Daddy

Harry

4y 4m

4y 4m

4y 6m

4y 1m

4y 1m

4y 2m

4y 4m

4y 4m

4y 6m

4y 6m

4y 8m

Figure 43: *(left)* Although Carol uses contouring for the limbs of her first conventional figures later she uses single lines. (AF65)

Figure 44: *(bottom)* The body and limbs of this girl's figure have been built up with multiple horizontal and vertical lines (aged 4 years 3 months). (AF22)

Figure 45: *(top)* Katrina regularly used a continuous outline to construct parts of her figures. (AF21)

8

Segmenting and

threading

Up until the age of about 5 or 6 years most children add each item to their figures in such a way that they have a segmented appearance (*see Figure 42*). But gradually they start to combine parts of the figure with a continuous contour; Jacqueline Goodnow (1977) called this 'threading'. In Amelia Fysh's collection, 5 per cent of the children combined the arms and the upper torso and 2 per cent combined the lower torso and the legs. In these cases the figures appear to be wearing a jumper or trousers, although we do not know whether the children intended the figures to be clothed. Four per cent of children drew a head and then used a continuous contour for the whole of the figure giving it a gingerbread man appearance. Two per cent drew a continuous contour around the arm and hand and 5 per cent drew one around the leg and foot. In the collection as a whole only 11 per cent of the children displayed any form of threading, although some children included more than one kind. (*See Figures 20, 32, 40, 41, 43, 45 and 50.*) Threading, then, is not particularly common in the nursery school. But, when I investigated threading in older children's drawings (Cox, 1993) I found that it had increased to 26 per cent among 5- to 6-year-olds, to 81 per cent among 7- to 8-year-olds and 96 per cent among 9- to 10-year-olds

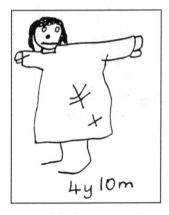

Figure 40a: *(Figure 40 shown complete on page 39)* Parts of figures begin to be combined with a continuous contour, called threading

Figure 42a: *(Figure 42 shown complete on page 43)* Items are added in such a way that figures have a segmented appearance

9

Gender in

children's

figures

Some researchers have found that girls tend to depict gender earlier than boys do (Papadakis-Michaelides, 1989; Willsdon, 1977). In their study of 1,600 boys and girls ranging in age from 3 years 6 months to 11 years 5 months and covering a variety of ethnic backgrounds, Ros Bradbury and Eleni Papadakis-Michaelides (1990) found that the female figures were drawn larger than the male figures particularly by the girls. Furthermore, the girls gave their female figures more 'gender-markers' than their male figures; female gender-markers are features such as hair-ribbons, jewellery, a waist and hips whereas males might have broad shoulders and large shoes.

Adonis Arazos and Alyson Davis (1989) asked a sample of 4- to 7-year-olds to draw both a boy and a girl. These researchers also found that female figures were drawn taller than the male figures. The older children, as expected, added more gender-markers than did the younger ones. But the most common item used to distinguish the figures even among the youngest children was hair length (long for a girl and short or even bald for a boy). Some children also drew trousers or triangular skirts. In a similar study, Ruth Sitton and Paul Light (1992) found the same pattern of development in Israeli children aged between 4 and 7 years and, in addition, noted that the extra items added by the older children included more elaborate hair-styles, hair-ribbons, high-heeled shoes and handbags.

Most of the children in these research studies have been older than those in the pre-school in the UK, where children normally move to the infants school at age 5. In the pre-school we are unlikely to see many obvious gender-markers in the children's drawings. In fact, only 9 per cent of Amelia Fysh's children drew figures which seem to display their gender, and even then we do not know for sure whether this was the children's intention or whether we are reading too much into the drawings. For example, some figures have long hair, earrings or a triangular skirt or dress suggesting that they may be females (*see Figures 31, 37, 39, 41 and 44*). Two figures which particularly appear to be female each has a triangular skirt and a bow in the hair (*see Figure 35*). Most of these figures which appear to display gender were drawn by girls. One exception is the set of figures drawn by Paul (*see Figure 46*): his last two figures drawn at nursery have trousers and are male.

Although the incidence of gender-markers is low in the drawings of Amelia Fysh's children this does not mean that these children were not capable of producing them. They may simply not have felt the need to do so. In the studies I have just mentioned, the researchers deliberately asked the children for a drawing of a male *and* a female. It is quite likely that this request contrasted the figures in the children's minds and increased the likelihood that they would add gender-differentiating features to make them more distinguishable.

3y 3m

3y 7m

3y 11m

4y 2m

4y 4m

4y 4m

4y 4m

'His hands are behind his back.'

4y 9m

4y 9m

4y 9m

The presence of genitalia (male and female sexual parts) in children's drawings is actually very rare, especially in figures they draw for adults. There are only two figures in Amelia Fysh's collection which might possibly display genitalia, both drawn by the same boy; such a judgment, however, is extremely uncertain since the scribbles are very ambiguous and there is no record of what the child actually intended them to be. Although I have collected thousands of children's figure drawings I have seen very few with genitalia and this has also been the experience of a number of other researchers (e.g., Ames and Ilg, 1963; Di Leo, 1970 and 1973; Koppitz, 1968; Rosen and Boe, 1968; Briggs and Lehmann, 1989).

Parents and teachers may be alarmed if they do see genitalia in their children's drawings, especially in the light of many recent sexual abuse cases in which some of the victims' drawings have displayed these graphic details. Joseph Di Leo (1970 and 1973) noted a 'generalised neglect of genitalia' (1970, p. 76) in the drawings of children from diverse backgrounds. He argued that if the depiction of genitalia is so rare then there must be some reason why the child has focused on them. The reason may not be that the child has been sexually abused; it could be that he or she is pre-occupied with this part of the body because of persistent bed-wetting or a recent or impending operation such as circumcision or herniorrhaphy. Even when we know that children have been sexually abused, however, very few actually depict genitalia in their drawings. In a study of thirty-six 3- to 7-year-olds, only three of those known to have been abused added genitalia (Hibbard, Roghmann and Hoekelman, 1987) and two out of twenty-one alleged but unsubstantiated cases did so. In a group of fifty-two comparison children with no history or suspicion of sexual abuse, one child drew genitalia. So, although there are very slightly more cases of genitalia depicted in the drawings of sexually abused children most of them omit the genitalia altogether. If we find that a child in the nursery is routinely drawing genitalia then we should be alert to that fact but very cautious that we do not jump to the wrong conclusion; other evidence must be sought. Conversely, the absence of genitalia in a drawing doesn't necessarily mean that the child hasn't been abused.

10

Orientation of

the figure

Figure 47: *(right)* Timothy's figures are frontal views. Later, at primary school, he draws in profile. (AF64a)

Most young children's figures are drawn full-face so that they look out directly at the viewer; the legs are straight and slightly apart and the arms are held away from the sides of the body. As Jacqueline Goodnow (1977) pointed out, children seem to go to great lengths to ensure that each body part has its own space; rarely does one part of the body overlap another part. This 'canonical' view of the figure is the best view in the sense that we can see that it has its full complement of facial features, two arms and two legs. By drawing this canonical view, children ensure that their figures are clearly recognizable. In Amelia Fysh's collection nearly all of the figures are frontal views; certainly no child drew a face in profile. Four per cent drew arms in such a way that the figure seemed to be viewed from the side and 15 per cent drew both feet pointing in the same direction, although we do not know whether the children intended the feet to be in profile. Profile figures, then, are very rare among nursery school children. One of Amelia Fysh's children, Timothy, developed normally in this respect and later, at the age of 9 years 10 months, drew profiles of his father, mother and sister (*see Figure 47*).

But to what extent are children actually capable of varying the orientation of their figures and drawing them in profile? When my students and I asked 344 children simply to 'draw a person' most of them drew a frontal view; only 14 per cent of 5- to 6-year-olds, 17 per cent of 7- to 8-year-olds and 21 per cent of 9- to 10-year-olds drew profile figures (Cox, 1993). When we asked another set of children – 345 of them – to draw a man running, the number who drew a profile figure increased to 57 per cent of 5- to 6-year-olds, 70 per cent of 7- to 8-year-olds and 84 per cent of 9- to 10-year-olds. Clearly, the older children are very successful when the instructions suggest a profile figure. They altered the orientation of the feet, the arms and the head, and in a few cases altered the shape of the torso. Some of the older children were also able to draw the figure so that part of an arm is hidden behind the torso or one leg is partly occluded by the other, but these adaptations do not occur much before the age of 9 or 10 years and even then only a minority of children attempt them. (*See Figure 48.*)

Rachel Moore and I (Cox and Moore, 1994) investigated this issue with even younger children. We included a group of thirty-three 4-year-olds who could draw a conventional figure and also a smaller group of eight tadpole-drawers, also 4-year-olds. In addition there was a group of 6-year-olds and a group of 8-year-olds. We asked the children to draw from a model. In fact they were asked to draw some pictures of 'Bob' the play person – a frontal view, a back view and a side view – and, in each case, Bob was placed in the appropriate orientation and remained visible throughout the drawing. Two of the tadpole-drawers and six of the 4-year-old

3y 8m

3y 9m

4y

4y 4m

4y 8m

4y 11m

5y

5y 2m

9y 10m

Figure 48: 'A man running' by 5-year-olds (upper), 7-year-olds (centre) and 9-year-olds (lower).

conventional drawers repeated their frontal canonical view for all three pictures of Bob. Most children, however, did not simply repeat the same figure and we can conclude that they were making some attempt to take account of Bob's three different orientations.

Most of the children omitted the facial features when Bob faced away from them; some of the older ones also tried to show how the feet were partially hidden in this orientation. The side view proved to be the most difficult and, not surprisingly, it was the older children who made more alterations to their normal figure (e.g., facial features, moulding of the head contour, drawing only one arm or one leg, pointing the feet to one side, partially hiding one leg behind the other). About 50 per cent of the 4-year-olds tried to alter their figure; they tended to make only one alteration such as the omission of an eye or an arm or the rotation of the whole figure on the page (*see Figure 49*). On the whole we cannot say that 4-year-olds were particularly successful at depicting a figure in profile but at least half of them recognized that they needed to alter their drawing and made an appropriate if limited attempt to do so.

I have already pointed out that children of all ages are more likely to draw a frontal view when they are simply asked to 'draw a person' and I have suggested that the reason for the predominance of this 'canonical' view is that it is the best or most typical view of a human figure which presents it in its most recognizable form. We have also seen, however, that many children, at least as young as 5 or even 4 years of age, are capable of changing the orientation of their figures. Jacqueline Goodnow (Goodnow, Wilkins and Dawes, 1986) has also discovered that children as young as 5 years are more 'experimental' in the drawings that they make spontaneously for themselves; for example, they may alter the basic structure of a figure or try to draw the figure in action. In contrast, the drawings made on request were in a frontal, 'still-life' style with greater attention to detail and proportion. In these request drawings there was an emphasis on people just 'being there' rather than people 'doing something'. In choosing to draw the more practised but perhaps more 'wooden' representation for an adult audience children may be responding to what they think adults will value, namely a figure in which all parts are 'present and correct'; normally, they may have far fewer encounters with adults who recognize and value their attempts to break away from a well-practised formula.

Figure 49: Children's drawings of a person from imagination and from three different views of a model.

11

What can figure drawings tell us about a child's intelligence?

It was very clear to the early investigators of children's drawings that as children get older they add more body parts to their figures and the proportions become more realistic. It also seemed to be the case that the more intellectually able children went through this process at an earlier age. At the beginning of the twentieth-century psychologists such as M.C. Schuyten (1904) had experimented with the possibility of devising a test of intelligence based on children's drawings, and slightly later Georges Rouma (1913) detailed a set of developmental stages specifically relating to children's human figure drawings. It was not until 1926, however, that the first 'test' was published. This was Florence Goodenough's Draw-a-Man test, initially based on the human figure drawings of nearly 4,000 children. Goodenough selected the man as the topic of the drawing since at that time there was greater uniformity in men's clothing as opposed to women's or children's. The Draw-a-Man test was updated by Dale Harris in 1963. Since that time Elizabeth Koppitz (1968) has also devised a similar kind of test, as has Jack Naglieri (1988). A recent survey of psychologists in the USA has found that these tests based on human figure drawings are among the top 10 assessment instruments (Archer, Maruish, Imhof and Piotrowski, in press). One of the attractions is that they are quick to administer. Also they can be given to groups, at least with older children. Further, it is believed that because of their non-verbal nature they may be less biased than many other tests, an important consideration when assessing children from different ethnic backgrounds.

Rather than collecting any pictures that the children happen to have completed it is important that the drawings are obtained under carefully monitored conditions. The instructions given by the test administrator must be carefully adhered to and a child must be doing his or her best. Obviously, if the child is not concentrating and produces a less detailed figure than usual then his ability in this test will be underestimated. Jacqueline Goodnow (Goodnow, Wilkins and Dawes, 1986) found that although children experimented more in their spontaneous drawings their figures were less detailed, less well-proportioned and 'practised' than when they drew for an adult on request; as a result, their spontaneous drawings attracted lower Draw-a-Man scores than did their requested figures. Of course, we will always find exceptions to these general tendencies. In Figure 50 we see that Ruth's spontaneous drawing of her teacher, completed at home, is much more detailed than the figures she drew on request around that time. As a general rule, though, in order to assess all children fairly it is important to ensure that the conditions in which their test drawings are collected are as similar as possible.

Figure 50: *(top right)* Ruth's spontaneous drawing of her teacher is more detailed than her usual figures at that time. (AF12)

Figure 51: *(bottom right)* This figure drawn by a girl, aged 5 years 9 months, scores 15 points (IQ 117) on Goodenough's Draw-a-Man test.

WHAT CAN FIGURE DRAWINGS TELL US ABOUT A CHILD'S INTELLIGENCE?

55

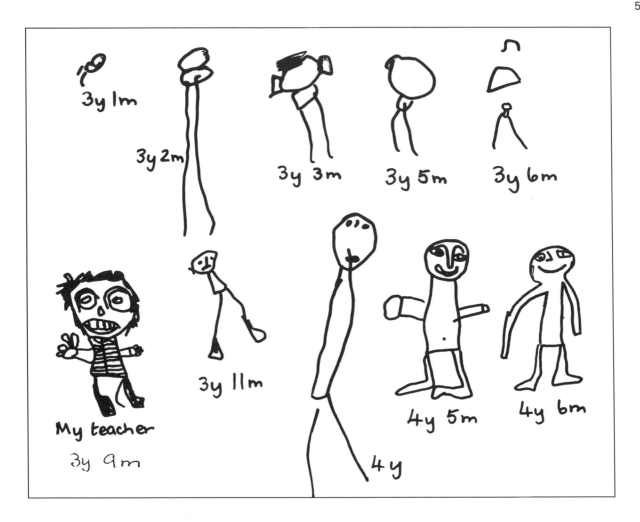

3y 1m

3y 2m

3y 3m

3y 5m

3y 6m

3y 11m

My teacher
3y 9m

4y

4y 5m

4y 6m

After the child has completed the drawing it is then 'scored' according to a checklist of items. In general, points are given for the presence of particular body parts, although they may also be given for the proportions of the figure or coordination of the lines. On the original Goodenough test a drawing can score up to 51 points. The girl aged 5 years 9 months who drew this figure (*see Figure 51*) scored 15 points for her picture. The figure has a head, containing eyes, nostrils and mouth. It also has hair. The torso is present and is longer than it is wide. The arms and legs are attached to the torso and the figure has hands. The figure appears to have clothes. The head and the arms are well proportioned. The total number of points is then compared with the 'norm' for the child's age group. In fact, this girl has scored 15 points, more than would be expected for her age group. The score can also be converted into an IQ score, using standardized charts, and again the girl is above average for her age with an IQ of 117.

The revised version of the Goodenough Draw-a-Man test (Harris, 1963) requires children to make three drawings (a man, a woman, and a self-drawing). Each figure can score up to 71 points. There are separate norms for male and female figures and assessors are advised to average the scores for a child's male and female figures in order to arrive at a more accurate estimate of achievement.

Girls tend to make their figures more detailed than boys and gain higher scores on average. This may reflect the faster developmental rate noted for girls over boys (Bee, 1995) which is also manifested in their verbal skills and arithmetic computation. In order to compensate for this difference in their drawings there are separate conversion tables for boys and girls in the revised version of the Draw-a-Man test (Harris, 1963). Thus, a boy who scores the same as a girl of the same age on the Draw-a-Man test will none the less be deemed to have a higher IQ when the score is converted.

Elizabeth Koppitz (1968) developed her Draw-a-Person test from the human figure drawings of a sample of nearly 2,000 children aged between 5 and 12 years. The child's figure drawing is scored according to a checklist of thirty developmental items (*see Table 1*) which Koppitz compiled from both the Goodenough-Harris test and her own experience of observing children's drawings.

Like the revised version of the Goodenough Draw-a-Man test Jack Naglieri's Draw-a-Person test (Naglieri, 1988) requires children to draw three figures (a man, a woman and oneself). Each figure can score 64 points based on the number of body parts included, the way the figure is elaborated and the connections between different body parts, as well as their proportions and locations. The scores for the three figures are combined and can be converted to a standard score (with an average of 100) using the tables provided. Naglieri used a sample of 2,622 children to develop the test and

Table 1: The 30 developmental items in Koppitz's Draw-a-Person test.

1.	Head	16.	Arms correctly attached to shoulders
2.	Eyes	17.	Elbows
3.	Pupils	18.	Hands
4.	Eyebrows or eyelashes	19.	Fingers
5.	Nose	20.	Correct numbers of fingers
6.	Nostrils	21.	Legs
7.	Mouth	22.	Legs in two dimensions
8.	Two lips	23.	Knees
9.	Ears	24.	Feet
10.	Hair	25.	Feet in two dimensions
11.	Neck	26.	Profile
12.	Body	27.	Clothing: one item or none
13.	Arms	28.	Clothing: two or three items
14.	Arms in two dimensions	29.	Clothing: four or more items
15.	Arms pointing downwards	30.	Good proportions

WHAT CAN FIGURE DRAWINGS TELL US ABOUT A CHILD'S INTELLIGENCE?

57

Figure 52: *(page 58)* This boy produced scribbles and some tadpole figures at nursery, but developed conventional figures later. (AF239)

these ranged from age 5 to 17 years.

These kinds of tests are reasonably reliable in the sense that the same child will produce similar figures on two different occasions (as long as the sessions are not too far apart in time) and also different test administrators will arrive at more or less the same score for the same child. There has been more disquiet, however, about the validity of the tests, that is how well they relate to scores on standard tests of intelligence. Whereas some studies have reported a reasonable or even a good relationship others have reported a rather poor one. These matters have been discussed recently in an article by Robert Motta, Steven Little and Michael Tobin (1993) and they conclude that 'human figure drawings are seriously flawed as a screening test for intellectual performance and are not useful as a predictor of academic achievement' (p. 167).

As well as this doubt about the tests there is also another issue regarding their usefulness. On the whole, they are based on work with older children, those of 5 years and over; as far as I know there has been no research into its possible use with pre-school children. In fact, I would argue that children's scores on a Draw-a-Man test in the pre-school are probably even less closely related to their general level of intelligence or intellectual achievement than in the primary school since the rate at which they adapt their figures is very varied at this young age, no doubt due to their individual characters as well as the many other different outside influences on them. In addition, it is often difficult to get these young children to produce 'the best picture you can' even when they are urged to do so. We must be very guarded therefore in making judgments since there may be reasons other than a lower general ability for a child's slower progress in drawing. Despite these doubts, I would still expect to see *some* positive relationship between pre-schoolers' drawings and their level of intellectual development. For example, I would guess that most of those children who are still scribbling at the age of 5 years are likely to be lower in general ability and, indeed, some of those who are still drawing tadpole figures at this age may also be lower than those who have moved on to a more conventional figure. There will always be exceptions, as Figure 52 shows: although this boy produced mainly scribbles and then tadpole figures in the nursery he developed normally and later was described as a 'good achiever'.

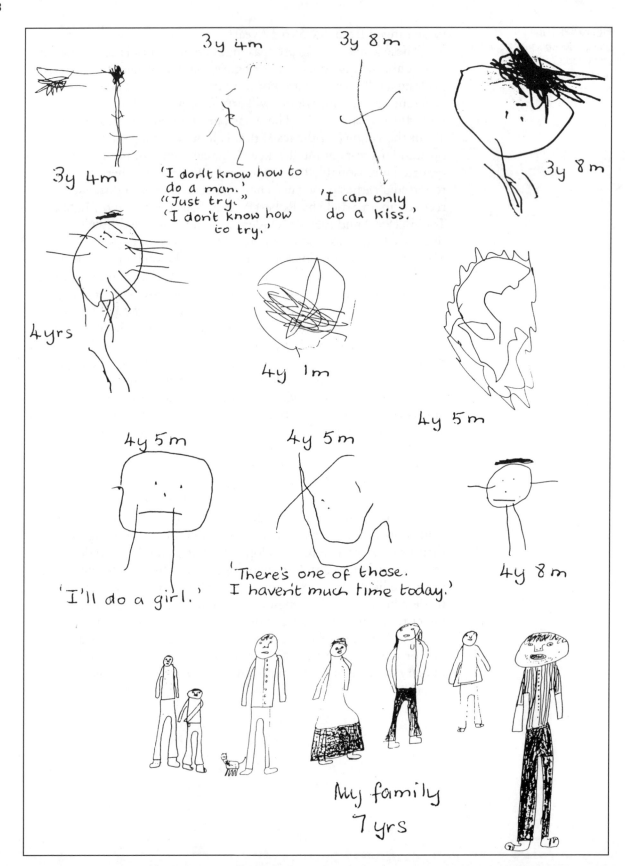

3y 4m

3y 8m

3y 4m

'I don't know how to
do a man.'
"Just try."
'I don't know how
to try.'

'I can only
do a kiss.'

3y 8m

4yrs

4y 1m

4y 5m

4y 5m

4y 5m

4y 8m

'I'll do a girl.'

'There's one of those.
I haven't much time today.'

My family
7 yrs

12

Children with an
intellectual
impairment or
learning
difficulties

Some children have a normal level of intellectual ability but have some degree of learning difficulty; dyslexia would be a clear example. Others have a lower level of intellectual functioning due to either some known or non-specific cause. Most research on children's drawing has been carried out with children who have a general intellectual impairment. I shall discuss first of all those studies in which the children's impairment had no known cause.

In fact there are different claims in the early literature on children's drawings as to whether the drawings of intellectually impaired children are noticeably different from those of normal children. Many researchers (e.g., Burt, 1921; Goodenough, 1926; Earl, 1933; Israelite, 1936; McElwee, 1934; Spoerl, 1940) argued that there are obvious differences, one of the most important being the unusual proportions of figures, lack of organization and addition of bizarre details drawn by the intellectually impaired children. Other researchers (e.g., Rouma, 1913), however, maintained that there is nothing particularly unusual about the drawings of intellectually impaired children, except that they resemble the figures drawn by younger children. In other words, intellectually impaired children perform at the level of children with a similar mental rather than chronological age.

Because of many methodological differences among the early studies it is difficult to decide from them which view is correct. But a number of more recent studies have helped us to decide the issue. First of all, Claire Golomb and Tracy Barr-Grossman (1977) studied the human figure drawings of a sample of children aged from 4 years 4 months to 13 years 1 month with IQs ranging from 40–76. These children had non-specific intellectual impairment, that is there was no known cause for their disability. The drawings were very similar to those of children who had the same mental age, although of course the latter were chronologically younger. The structure of the figures was similar with no noticeable problems of organization, proportion or addition of bizarre details. The only difference was that the intellectually impaired children with a mental age of 4 or 5 years drew slightly more details than did the normal children of that age. In a study of fifteen 9-year-old children who were severely intellectually impaired (a measured IQ below 50 and a mental age of 3 years 9 months) Claire Howarth and I also found that these children perform at a level similar to their mental age rather than their chronological age (Cox and Howarth, 1989); only one child drew a conventional figure, nine drew tadpole forms and five drew non-recognizable figures. (*See Figure 53.*)

More recently one of my students, Samantha Cotgreave, asked teachers of normal children and teachers of children who are moderately intellectually impaired to see if they could distinguish the drawings completed by normal and intellectually impaired

Figure 53: Figures drawn by a child with severe learning difficulties: (a) a pre-school child (b) and a child at primary school (c).

Figure 54: *(page 61)* Alan stayed at nursery school for an extra term before moving to infants school; later, he attended a special school for the mentally handicapped. (AF14)

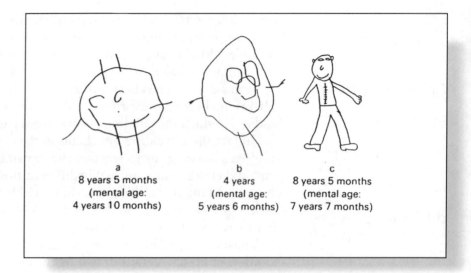

a
8 years 5 months
(mental age:
4 years 10 months)

b
4 years
(mental age:
5 years 6 months)

c
8 years 5 months
(mental age:
7 years 7 months)

children. The drawings were completed by eighteen 10-year-old children with a mental age of 6 years, eighteen normal 6-year-olds and eighteen normal 10-year-olds. We jumbled up the fifty-four drawings and asked twelve teachers to sort them into a 'normal 6-year-old', a 'normal 10-year-old' and an 'intellectually impaired' pile. All twelve teachers completed the task separately. They could easily identify the figures drawn by the older, normal children. However, they were no better than chance at identifying the 6-year-olds' figures and the figures drawn by the intellectually impaired children.

We can make a tentative conclusion that intellectually impaired children generally draw in accord with their mental age and that their pictures are not markedly different from those drawn by younger, normal children. Of course, we recognize that we have carried out this exercise with only a very small number of teachers and we would wish to extend it to a much larger number before coming to more than a tentative conclusion.

On the whole, research studies have investigated intellectually impaired children who are, chronologically, much older than those in the pre-school, and to my knowledge there is no systematic study of the drawing skills of very young ones. In Amelia Fysh's collection of drawings there is a set (*see Figure 54*) drawn by a little boy called Alan who seemed to be slow in his development and, in fact, stayed on for an extra term in the nursery before being transferred to an infants school for a trial period; subsequently he attended a special school for the mentally handicapped. Alan loved dressing-up games and joined in a Christmas play under the guidance of a talented reception class teacher. At 4 years 8 months his figure is little more than a 'tadpole' and his control over the pencil was not very assured. He did, however, show some progress with a more conventional figure over the next year.

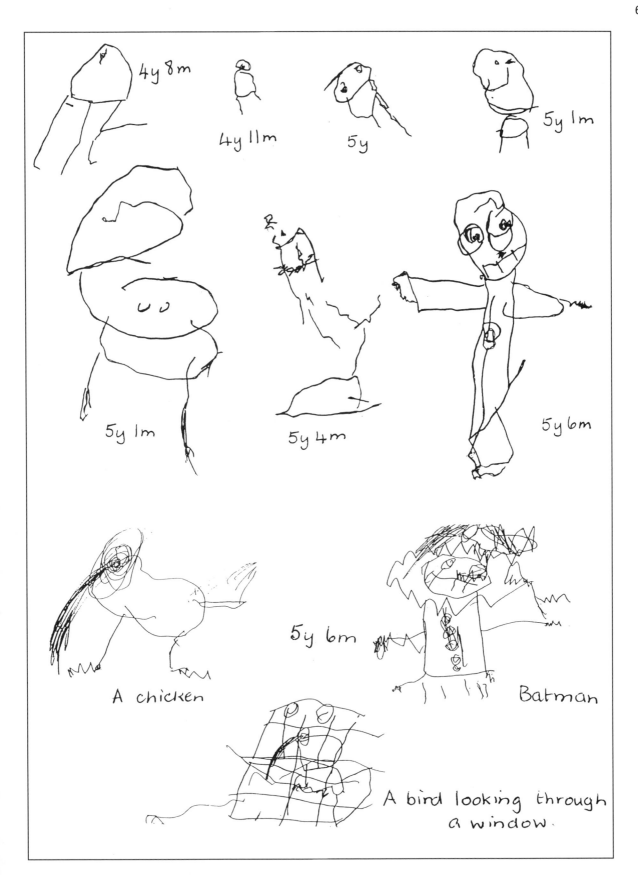

4y 8m

4y 11m

5y

5y 1m

5y 1m

5y 4m

5y 6m

A chicken

5y 6m

Batman

A bird looking through a window.

Figure 55: *(right)* Sharon who has Down's Syndrome, attended nursery school between the ages of 3 and 6 years. (AF15)

In the collection there is also a set of drawings completed by a child with Down's Syndrome (*see Figure 55*). Sharon arrived at the nursery shortly after her third birthday and stayed there until she was 6. Her speech was very poor but her span of attention was good and she enjoyed a variety of activities. She was not particularly nimble with her fingers and had difficulty in tying her shoe-laces but she enthusiastically tried every sort of creative material offered in the nursery. Her drawings are very similar to many early productions of normal children but we can see how the development is slow and spreads out over a much longer period of time; Sharon was nearly 6 years old before she drew a figure which we can vaguely recognize and she was drawing tadpole figures at the age of 6 years 9 months. I should emphasize that there is a huge variability among Down's Syndrome children in terms of intellectual functioning, ranging from very low to low-normal in measured IQ, and indeed in the level of a variety of specific skills. So it would be inappropriate to take Sharon's case as typical of all Down's Syndrome children.

There are other, more social, reasons why some children may be slower in their development. In Amelia Fysh's collection there are a few sets of drawings by children who came from deprived or disturbed home backgrounds and, in some cases, their attendance at nursery was very irregular. Andy had a very disturbed home life: his father was often violent and his mother was nervous and anxious. The scenes at home frightened the children and the mother could see no way out of the difficulties at that time. Andy was rather reticent with the nursery staff although he cooperated with other children in group activities. We can see the early elements of a figure emerging in some of his drawings (*see Figure 56*) but his development was slow and uneven and he had still not developed very clearly recognizable figures when he left the nursery at the age of 5 years.

As a toddler Terry was brought into the nursery by his mother when she delivered and collected his older brother. When he first attended the nursery himself he looked puzzled and confused. He fitted in well with outdoor activities but was less sure of himself indoors. He seemed to be looking for reassurance, which was readily given by the staff, and needed a lot of guidance in the use of everyday materials. He seemed to be unused to conversation and was singled out for extra language stimulation. Although he was cooperative the nursery staff felt that he made little progress despite this extra attention. We can see some possible elements of a figure in some of Terry's drawings but he did not produce any clearly recognizable figures during his time at the nursery (*see Figure 57*); he left at the age of 4 years 7 months.

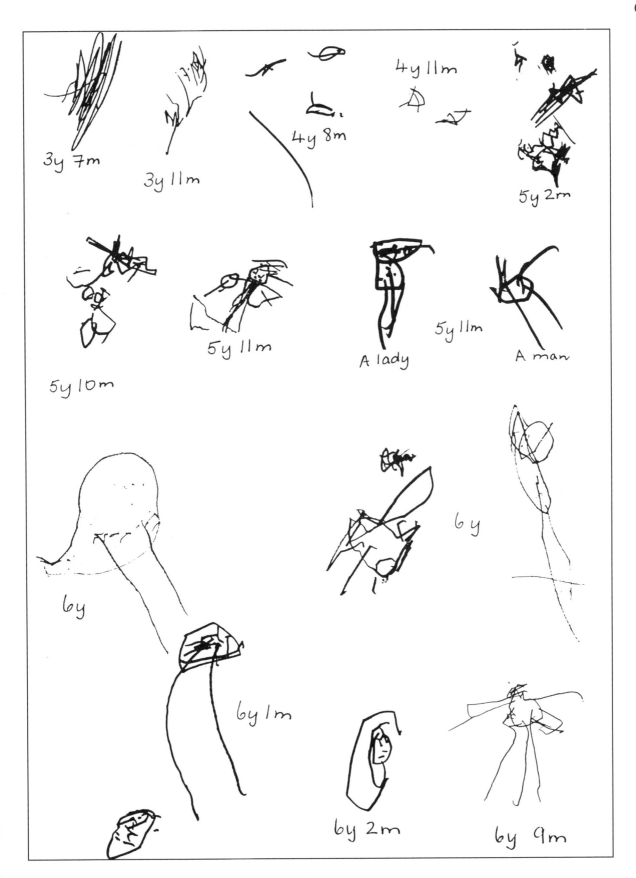

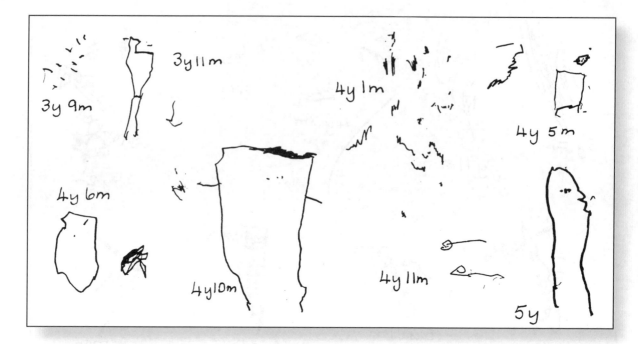

3y 9m

3y 11m

4y 1m

4y 5m

4y 6m

4y 10m

4y 11m

5y

Figure 56: Andy had a very disturbed home life and erratic attendance at nursery school. His development was slow and his figures are not easily recognizable. (AF198)

Figure 57: *(page 65)* Terry's figures were not easily recognizable during his time at nursery school. (AF61a)

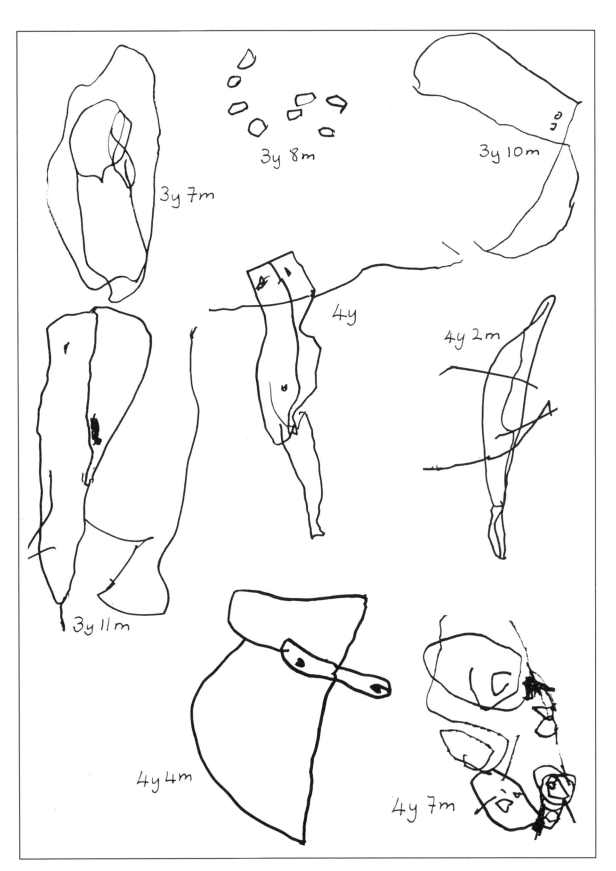

3y 8m

3y 10m

3y 7m

4y

4y 2m

3y 11m

4y 4m

4y 7m

13

Children with

physical

disabilities

Some children with physical disabilities may have a normal rate of intellectual development whereas others may develop more slowly or at least more slowly in areas where their physical disability is an obvious handicap. Whereas some of these children have no difficulties with drawing, others do simply because they cannot manipulate the pencil or crayon with the same ease as able-bodied children, and yet others may make slower progress with drawing along with other skills. There is actually little research on the drawings produced by children with physical disabilities. I shall describe some examples from Amelia Fysh's collection, although with such a small sample covering a wide range of disabilities it is difficult to make any generalized comments.

Tina had 'petit mal' epilepsy. She settled into the nursery quite normally and was cheerful and lively. Her hand–eye coordination was good; she mastered jigsaws and constructive toys and liked painting with a brush and also finger painting. The development of her drawings was rather slow however (*see Figure 58*); on the whole she was making scribbles or tentative shapes in the nursery and only began to draw what looks like a 'tadpole' right at the end of her time there. In the third term of the infants school she was drawing tadpole figures at the age of 5 years 8 months.

A hyperactive boy, called Graham, found great difficulty in attending to any activity for more than a minute or so. He flitted from one thing to the next and was unable to cooperate with other children. He was only contained within play situations through the skill of the nursery staff. His progress was very slow and this is

Figure 58: Tina, with petit mal epilepsy, did not draw recognizable figures until she went to infants school. (AF9)

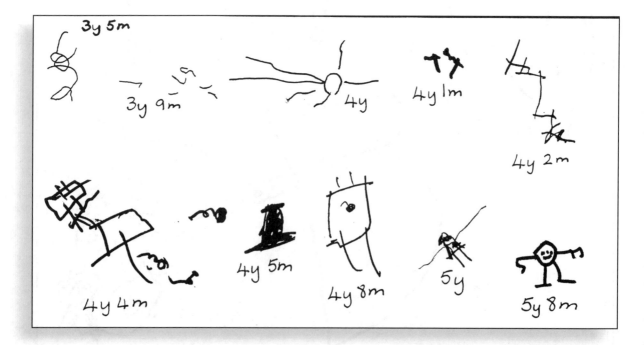

3y 5m

3y 9m

4y

4y 1m

4y 2m

4y 4m

4y 5m

4y 8m

5y

5y 8m

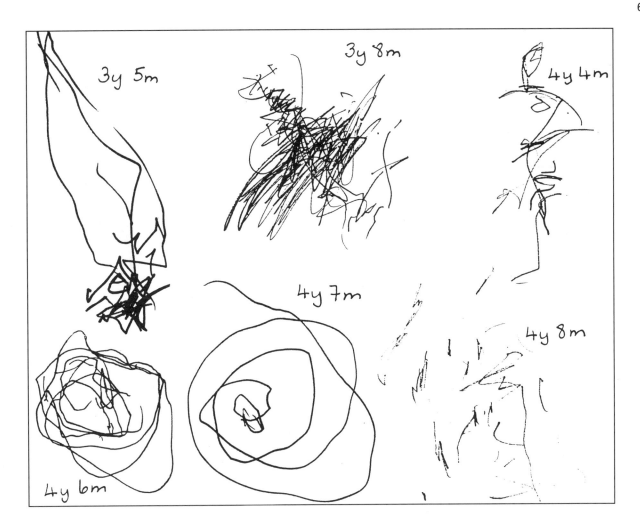

3y 5m

3y 8m

4y 4m

4y 7m

4y 8m

4y 6m

Figure 59: Over a 15-month period in nursery school, Graham produced various types of scribble. (AF34)

reflected in his scribbles (*see Figure 59*); however, we can see some experimentation in the kinds of scribbles he produced over a 15-month period.

Jane had diabetes and refused sugary party food or other treats with dignity and self-control. She seemed a sad little girl, was quiet and shy and clung closely to an adult for approval. She played a lot on her own but she was encouraged to join in group activities and story time. She used creative materials quite skilfully and although her small set of figure drawings covers only seven months they show normal development (*see Figure 60*); by the age of 4 years 7 months she is drawing a conventional figure and at 5 years 1 month she has started to embellish it with hair (or a hat) and buttons.

Michael was suffering from ataxia (difficulty in coordinating bodily movements) and also had a severe hearing deficit. He attended the partially hearing unit in the morning and arrived at the nursery for the afternoon session. His speech was almost unintelligible but, despite this, he got on well with other children

4y 7m

4y 8m

4y 11m

5y 1m

Figure 60: Despite her
diabetes and shyness
Jane's use of creative
materials was quite skilful.
(AF108)

Figure 60: Despite her
diabetes and shyness
Jane's use of creative
materials was quite skilful.
(AF108)

Figure 61: *(page 69)*
Although his movements
were jerky, due to ataxia,
Michael produces a tadpole
figure at age 4 years 1
month and a conventional
figure at 4 years 8 months.
(AF237)

and joined in group activities and listened to stories with great
attention. In spite of his jerky movements he was able to master
tools and creative materials and greatly enjoyed painting and
building. Michael's figure drawings clearly show his difficulty in
controlling a pencil (*see Figure 61*). Nonetheless, he produces a
tadpole figure at just over 4 years of age and a conventional figure at
4 years 8 months.

Joanna was partially sighted due to albinism. She played happily
with other children and was confident with all indoor and outdoor
activities. Never the less, she had to peer closely to do her drawing
and painting and held books very close to her face. Joanna enjoyed
music and, much later, at the age of 18 she took a music degree; she
played the piano, the violin and the viola and also composed. She
won a music scholarship which was presented by the former Prime
Minister, Edward Heath. Joanna's set of drawings (*see Figure 62*)
shows that before the age of 4 years she was drawing conventional
figures, even though a tadpole figure crops up a couple of times at
age 4 and 4 years 2 months. Her figures are boldly drawn and quite
detailed, and at age 4 years 1 month she deliberately starts to shade
in the clothing saying, 'It's a Mummy. I am putting clothes on. She
will catch cold if I don't'. Despite her visual handicap Joanna's
drawings not only reflect a normal intellectual development but an
ability above average for her age. She continued to draw well as her
'family portrait' at age 12 shows.

Rachel was handicapped by spina bifida and hydrocephalus.
Although she was paralysed from the waist down she could shuffle

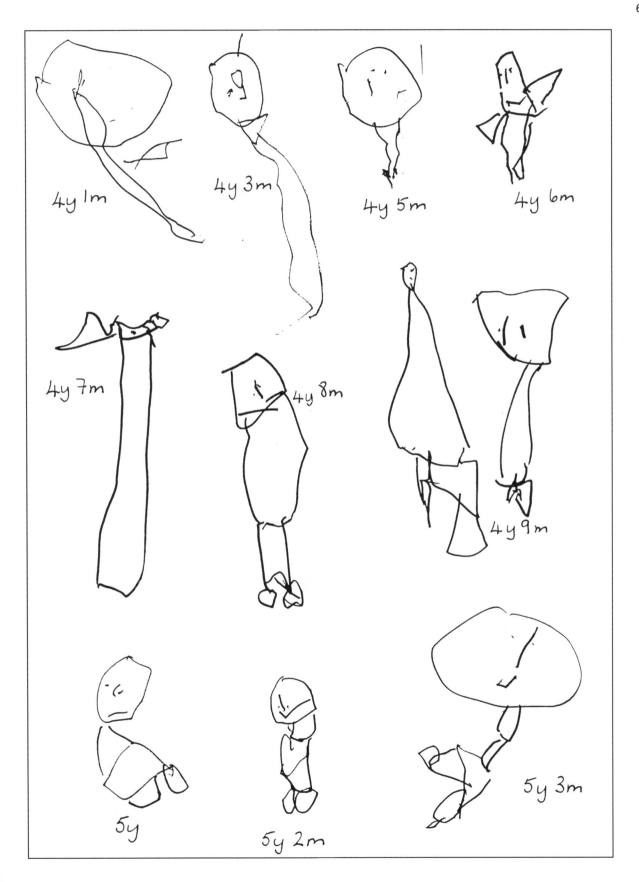

4y 1m

4y 3m

4y 5m

4y 6m

4y 7m

4y 8m

4y 9m

5y

5y 2m

5y 3m

3y 11m

4y

4y 1m

4y 1m

4y 2m

Mummy   Baby   Daddy

4y 3m

4y 6m

12y

Figure 62: *(left)* Joanna was partially sighted, due to albinism, but her drawing reflects her above-average ability. (AF53)

Figure 63: *(page 72)* Rachel is paralysed from the waist down but was able to draw normally and paint at the easel. (AF56)

Figure 64: *(page 73)* Samantha mixes tadpole figures, transitional and conventional forms during her time at the nursery. (AF57)

along on her bottom and was agile in her wheelchair. In her callipers she was not so free to move but she said, 'I am standing up like the others', and she was able to paint at the easel. In every way Rachel was normal except for the fact that she could not walk unaided. She began to draw conventional figures at the age of 4 years 8 months (*see Figure 63*).

Like Rachel, Samantha was also handicapped by spina bifida and hydrocephalus. At nursery she used a wheelchair and was very mobile, often giving rides to other children who sat in a truck tied on behind. She also had callipers and used sticks for part of every day. Samantha joined in enthusiastically in nearly all the nursery's activities. She sang with gusto and in *The Grand Old Duke of York* held up her sticks high for 'when they were up they were up'. Samantha's figures are quite variable: we can identify tadpole figures, transitional and conventional figures (*see Figure 64*). Interestingly, in the last group, drawn at age 5 years 3 months, Mummy and Daddy both appear to have bodies whereas Samantha and her brother do not.

Jonathan had a congenital deformity: his arms were rather short and he had only three fingers on each hand. Despite his handicap he was a normal little boy and readily engaged in all the activities in the nursery including model making, painting and crayoning. His achievements were a source of inspiration to the staff and satisfaction for himself. Not surprisingly his drawings reflect his difficulty in controlling a pencil (*see Figure 65*). Never the less, he introduced some of the elements needed for a figure in his first drawing here at the age of 3 years 9 months: he is able to draw both straight lines and make rather rough but closed shapes. His first tadpole figure appears when he was 4. It is not clear whether the figure he drew at 4 years 11 months is a conventional one but the next one, at 5 years 3 months, certainly is.

Jamie suffered from osteo genesis imperfecta (brittle bones); he was severely handicapped and had very short limbs. When he first came to the nursery at the age of 3 he was confined to a pram on which a tray was fixed in order to support materials for him to play with. Later, he was in a pushchair although the staff exercised their ingenuity in many ways in order to include him in all the children's activities. Although he sustained no broken bones at the nursery he did arrive in plaster from time to time and was often in pain and discomfort. Despite all this he enjoyed being involved in group activities and games. He is still remembered for his 'great personality', his verbal skill and, unlike most 4- to 5-year-olds, his ability to sing in tune.

Amelia Fysh notes that despite his handicap Jamie had a talent for drawing (*see Figure 66*). He experimented with squiggles and lines over a six-month period and was producing conventional

72

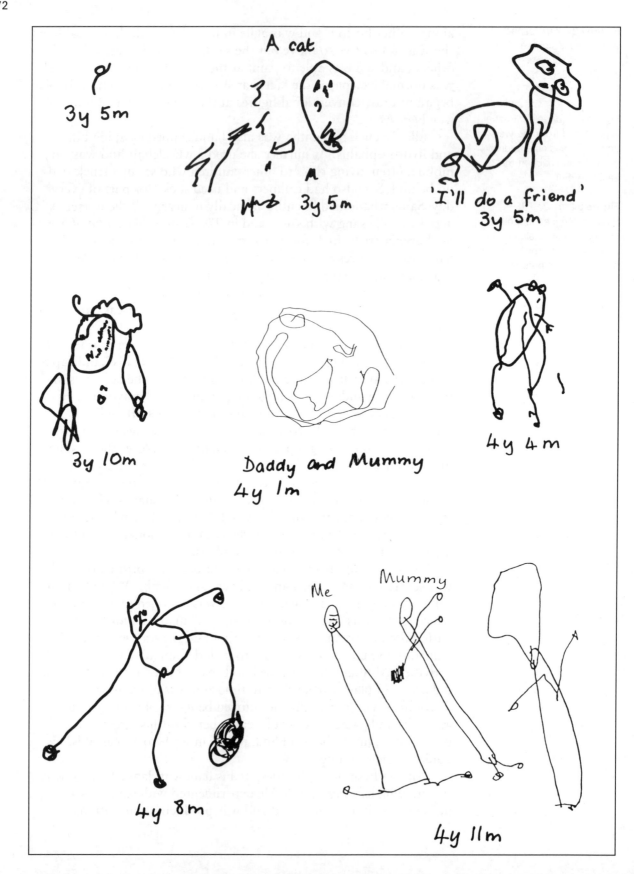

A cat

3y 5m

3y 5m

'I'll do a friend'
3y 5m

3y 10m

Daddy and Mummy
4y 1m

4y 4m

4y 8m

Me   Mummy

4y 11m

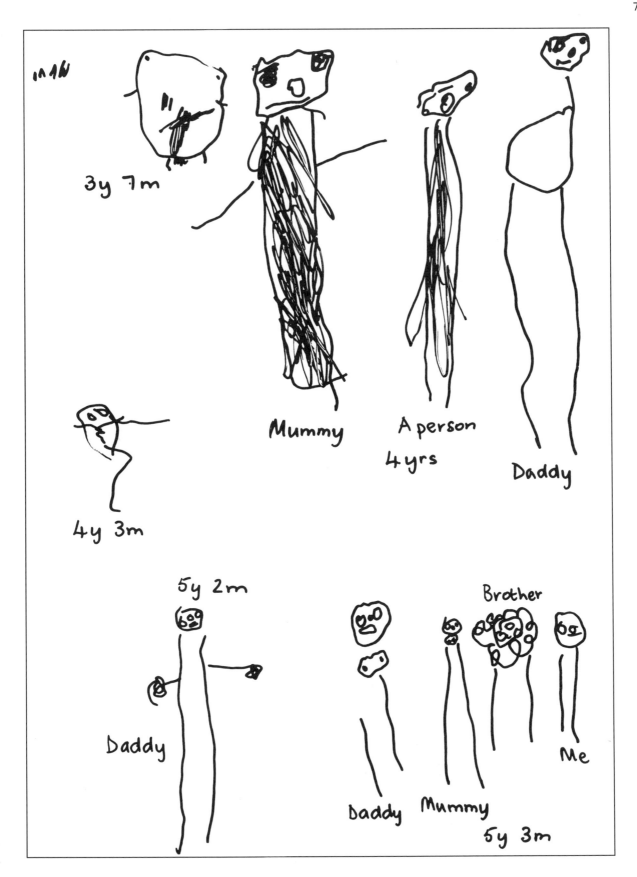

3y 7m

Mummy

A person

4yrs

Daddy

4y 3m

5y 2m

Brother

Daddy

Daddy   Mummy

Me

5y 3m

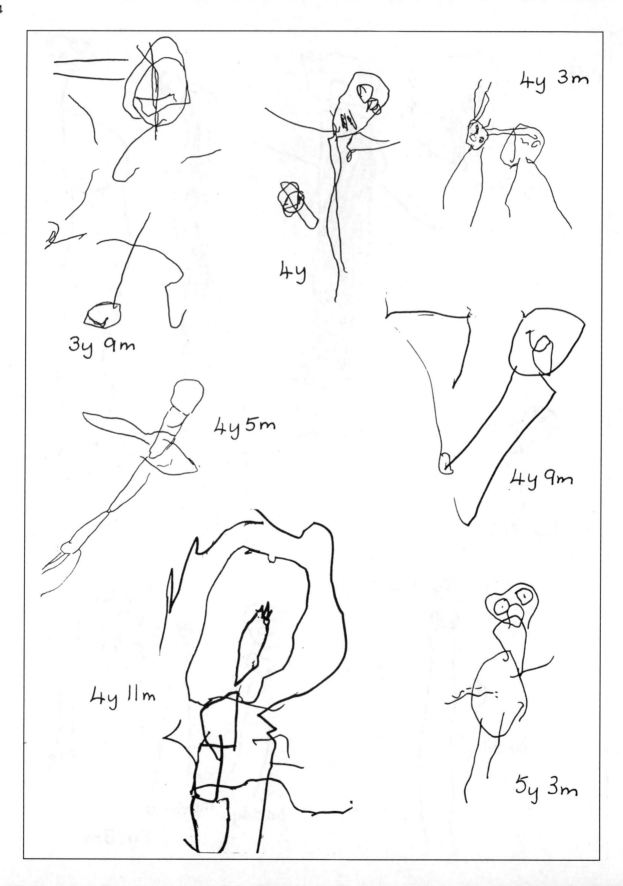

4y 3m

4y

3y 9m

4y 5m

4y 9m

4y 11m

5y 3m

Figure 65: *(left)* Jonathan, with a deformity of the hands, had some difficulty in controlling the pencil but the structure of his figures develops normally. (AF38)

Figure 66: *(page 76)* Jamie, who had brittle bones and was severely physically handicapped, was a talented drawer. (AF30)

Figure 67: *(page 77)* These delightful pictures reflect Jamie's love for drawing. (AF30)

figures at the age of 4 years 7 months. Interestingly, there is no tadpole figure in this set; we do not know whether Jamie simply missed out this stage or whether he drew tadpole figures at another time or at home. As Jamie had a limited reach and found it difficult to grip the pencil it is not surprising that the lines of his figures have a wavy quality; never the less, his physical problem did not prevent him from developing his drawing in a remarkably normal way. His earliest recognizable figures were drawn spontaneously rather than on request (*see Figure 67*). He loved to draw incidents such as 'Me catching a butterfly' and he produced some delightful drawings of animals after a visit to a nearby zoo.

When he was 5 years old Jamie went to Stoke Mandeville Hospital school in the mornings and came back to the nursery in the afternoons. He attended a village school, part-time, at the age of 6 and continued there until, sadly, he died at the age of 6 years 10 months.

It is not surprising that we should see a slight delay in a child with damage to the arms and hands (*see Figure 65*) nor that a hyperactive child with a severely limited concentration span should progress slowly (*see Figure 59*). But it is not so clear in the case of the child with petit mal epilepsy (*see Figure 58*), unless her attention was constantly being interrupted by her condition. Interpretation is always difficult with single cases since we cannot say for sure whether a delay is related to the disability itself or whether there were other contributory reasons. We would need to study a much larger sample of children with each kind of disability in order to come to any firm conclusions. In general, though, the examples I have described suggest that even children with quite serious physical disabilities are not necessarily delayed in their drawing development if they are otherwise intellectually unimpaired.

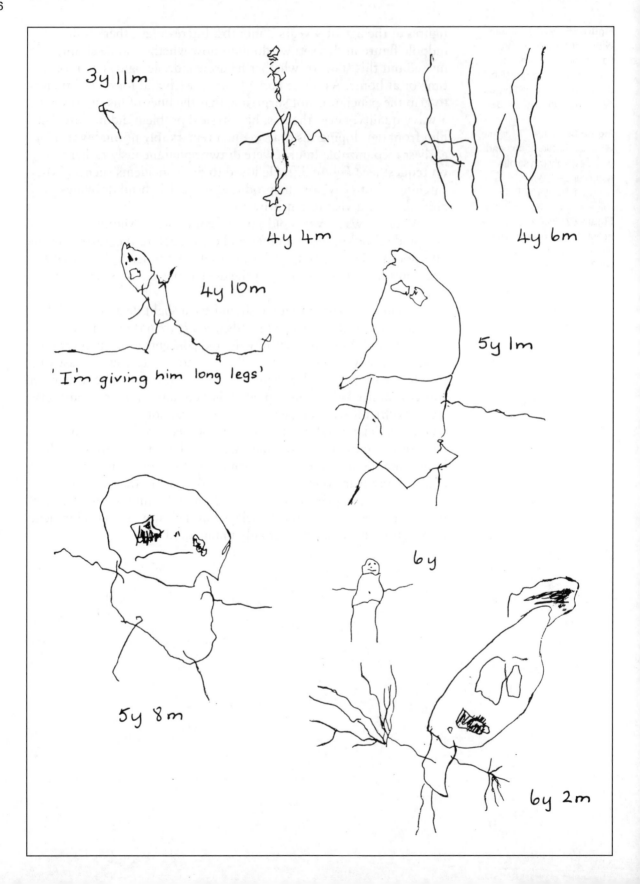

3y 11m

4y 4m

4y 6m

4y 10m

'I'm giving him long legs'

5y 1m

5y 8m

6y

6y 2m

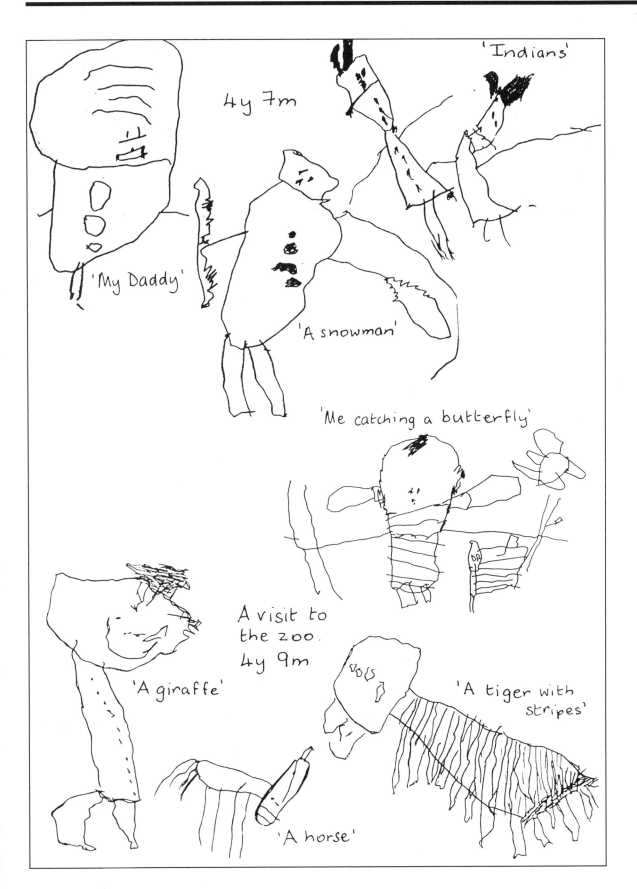

'Indians'

4y 7m

'My Daddy'

'A snowman'

'Me catching a butterfly'

A visit to
the zoo.
4y 9m

'A giraffe'

'A tiger with
stripes'

'A horse'

14

Can drawings tell us about a child's personality or emotional stability?

Many people believe that children's drawings are so natural and spontaneous that they provide us with a 'window on the mind'. Inspired by the new and exciting field of psychoanalysis early in the twentieth century many therapists turned to children's drawings which they believed could provide this window into the child's mind. Since their drawings are supposedly a product of self-expression, totally uncontaminated by the surrounding culture, it is often claimed that it should be possible for us to interpret the pictures and discover something about a child's personality or emotional state. One of the most widely used approaches in clinical practice has been Karen Machover's Draw-a-Person test (1949). First of all, the child is asked to 'draw a person' or to 'draw somebody'. This figure is presumed to represent the child himself. Then the child is asked to draw another person (of the opposite sex to the first one) on a second sheet of paper. The second figure is supposed to represent an important person in the child's life and to indicate something about his relationship to that person. The clinician interprets the figures, taking into account the particular body parts included or omitted, their size and shape, their position on the page, the quality of the line, the amount of erasure, and so on. The interpretation is from a psychoanalytic orientation which imbues each segment or line of the drawing with symbolic meaning. For example, shading and erasure is said to indicate a sense of weakness and heavy pressure on the pencil to indicate a need for social participation. An oversized head suggests intellectual aspiration, pronounced ears reflect over sensitivity to criticism, the omission of pupils from the eyes indicates self-centredness, and so on.

As well as their use by therapists human figure drawings are also widely used by school psychologists in the USA for assessing children's social emotional functioning (Prout, 1983) and to assess personality (Goh and Fuller, 1983). The kind of projective technique advocated by Machover is often used in their interpretation.

This approach to children's drawings has largely ignored how normal children's drawings develop and often attributes a 'psychological' meaning when the child is simply grappling with the problem of how to draw. In addition, the approach has also ignored the way that culture influences children's drawings, particularly during the school years. Many research studies have attempted to test the claims put forward by Karen Machover and there have been a number of reviews of them (Swensen, 1957 and 1968; Roback, 1968; Klopfer and Taulbee, 1976; Kahill, 1984; Motta, Little and Tobin, 1993). They have all concluded that there is little if any value in the projective approach; in particular, judgments based on a single feature, such as the way the head is drawn or the pressure on

CAN DRAWINGS TELL US ABOUT A CHILD'S PERSONALITY OR EMOTIONAL STABILITY?

79

the pencil, are very unreliable.

Despite this condemnation many psychotherapists and art therapists who work with children still continue to make these projective interpretations of their pictures. One psychotherapist (also trained as an art therapist) commented recently, 'Like dreams they [children's drawings] are an expression of their unconscious mind, something which is not normally accessible' (Wilson, 1993, p. 37). Asked to analyse some children's drawings for a popular magazine this psychotherapist interpreted the drawings, presumably without knowing anything about the identity of the figures, the order in which they were drawn or the context of the drawing session itself. Commenting on 3-year-old Ian's picture (*see Figure 68*) she says, 'This is a typical drawing for his age, consisting of two figures with just a head and a body of sorts. If he's drawing his parents, it could be he feels one parent is much stronger than the other' (p. 36). Unless we are supplied with further information we cannot know who the figures were meant to be; they may not be Ian's parents at all. Even if they were his parents one figure may have ended up smaller than the other simply because there was insufficient space on the page after the first one had been completed. The second example (*see Figure 69*), drawn by Michael aged almost 5 years, is interpreted thus, 'The whole drawing smacks of insecurity and if it's a figure of his family with his father in the centre, it looks as though he has represented himself as exceedingly small. This could denote a feeling of helplessness' (p. 39). Again we should be sceptical. We do not know who the figures were meant to be and there may be many reasons why the figure on the left-hand side is relatively small.

As well as a checklist of thirty items devised to measure a child's intellectual maturity Elizabeth Koppitz (1968) also listed thirty items that would indicate a child's emotional adjustment (*see Table 2*). These items include some of those in the Machover test – shading of face, big hands, no arms, etc. – but they are not on the whole given a symbolic meaning. Koppitz also emphasizes that it is not any one particular item that matters but the total number of them and that emotionally unstable children will exhibit more in their drawings than will normal children. Even so, as Koppitz herself acknowledges, we must also take account of the age of the child. Whereas the absence of a torso or arms in a 7-year-old's figure would be unusual it would be quite normal for a 3- or 4-year-old. In fact, when Koppitz compared the human figure drawings of normal and emotionally disturbed children she did not include the under-5s. Clearly, her test is aimed at older children who normally include a large number of body parts in their figures and who have begun to adapt the shape and proportion of them.

The usefulness of Koppitz's test, as with any test, is whether it

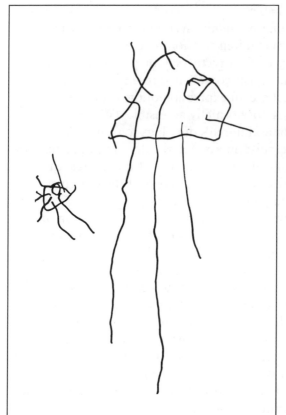

Figure 68: *(left)* Two figures drawn by 3-year-old Ian.

Figure 69: *(right)* Figures drawn by Michael, aged almost 5 years.

Table 2: The 30 emotional indicators in Koppitz's Draw-a-Person test.

really does help distinguish those children with emotional difficulties from normal children. Elizabeth Koppitz herself studied a group of seventy-six 5- to 12-year-olds who were judged by their teachers to be well adjusted. Their human figure drawings were compared with those drawn by a group of seventy-six children who attended a child guidance clinic. Fifty-eight (76 per cent) of the normal group drew

1. Poor integration of parts	16. Big hands
2. Shading of face	17. Hands cut off
3. Shading of body and/or limbs	18. Legs pressed together
4. Shading of hands and/or neck	19. Genitals
5. Gross asymmetry of limbs	20. Monster or grotesque figure
6. Slanting figure	21. Three or more figures spontaneously drawn
7. Tiny figure	22. Clouds
8. Big figure	23. No eyes
9. Transparencies	24. No nose
10. Tiny head	25. No mouth
11. Crossed eyes	26. No body
12. Teeth	27. No arms
13. Short arms	28. No legs
14. Long arms	29. No feet
15. Arms clinging to body	30. No neck

CAN DRAWINGS TELL US ABOUT A CHILD'S PERSONALITY OR EMOTIONAL STABILITY?

81

no emotional indicators whereas only seven (9 per cent) children in the clinical group drew none. Among the normal children, fourteen drew one emotional indicator and four drew two. In the clinical group, fifty-seven children (75 per cent) drew two or more emotional indicators.

If children are emotionally disturbed we might expect that they may also be retarded in their development, temporarily at least. If this is the case then it may be that emotionally disturbed children will draw a figure more in keeping with their mental age rather than their chronological age. Recently, one of my students, Michelle Catte, compared the drawings of primary school children who had been referred to the pupil support service for emotional/behavioural problems with those of another well-adjusted group who were younger but had a similar mental age. She found that there was no difference in the number of emotional indicators between the two groups. She also asked three people who are very familiar with children's drawings to see if they could tell which were the drawings completed by the emotionally disturbed children and which were done by normal children. These 'judges' could not reliably tell the difference. It seems, then, that emotionally disturbed children may simply be retarded in the way they draw, retarded in the sense of drawing like a younger child; apart from that, their drawings are not noticeably unusual.

Overall, then, although there is great interest in what children's drawings can tell us about the children themselves the research suggests that this approach is not very reliable and may be inappropriate for very young children. I believe that we would be reading far too much into their drawings if we pursue this approach, at least with our present state of knowledge. Perhaps the best use for human figure drawings in clinical settings is as an 'ice-breaker' activity. Often, children who are disturbed or withdrawn cannot or will not easily talk about their problems but the process of drawing may help them begin to express themselves and also provide a focus for discussion with a caring and interested adult.

15

Giving

a helping hand

Does intervention stifle creativity?

Many parents and teachers believe that they should not intervene in their children's artwork since the whole point of it is concerned with self-expression. Furthermore, they often fear that interference may stifle children's creativity and even cause psychological damage. Where did these ideas come from? They can be traced back to a number of influential authors. One was Franz Cisek working in Vienna in the 1890s and later (reported by Viola, 1936) who became interested in children's drawing and painting and set up children's art classes. He later became known as 'the father of child art' although a number of other people might also be justified in claiming this title, for example the American, Earl Barnes (1893), and the Italian, Corrado Ricci (1887). Franz Cisek believed that children's artwork is universal and spontaneous and that it can and should develop effortlessly into the creativity of the adult artist, if it is left uncontaminated by the cultural conventions we normally try to impose on it both through our expectations and teaching. Many parents and teachers have taken this to mean that we should certainly not show children how to draw and should perhaps even refrain from commenting on a child's drawing lest any apparent criticism stifles the child's future creativity.

Later, in the twentieth century, the Austrian-American art educator Viktor Löwenfeld (1939 and 1957) reiterated these views, making it clear that the spontaneous artwork flowing from young children should be regarded in almost a sacred way and should not be tampered with at all. He appealed to teachers never to allow children to copy the work of others lest their own innate and unique creativity is suppressed.

These art educators were probably reacting to what they saw as the over-formal, technique-led approach to art which was dominant in the nineteenth century and continued in the twentieth century in the elementary schools; basically, children were given instruction as early as possible and drilled in copying three-dimensional models or other drawings and paintings. But not everyone accepted the newer, *laissez-faire* approach. In fact, a number of artists, art critics and historians were openly critical, doubting that there could ever be such a thing as an 'innocent eye' and claiming that all art is based largely on what has been achieved before (see Wilson and Wilson, 1977). Indeed, one of the chief ways in which most artists, at least in the past, have developed their talent has been by the careful copying of the work of other acclaimed masters, yet this practice has not been a barrier to their own subsequent creativity.

Even when children are not taught to copy, however, their drawings are not necessarily completely new and creative. In fact, rather than working out their own graphic images many of them prefer to copy the images they see around them – in comics, books, television and other media sources – and it is really not possible to stop them. Brent and Marjorie Wilson interviewed 147 teenagers about the sources of the graphic images in their pictures. They found that nearly all of them could be traced to the illustrations and photographs of popular culture available at school or at home. So, far from being keen to develop their own completely novel images children will often use existing sources.

Brent and Marjorie Wilson (1984) have also investigated the imagery used by younger children in different societies, showing that their images are not universally the same but are very much influenced by the particular culture they find themselves in. Interestingly, in some non-western cultures with fewer multi-media influences the range of images in children's pictures is *less* not more inventive. It seems to be a myth that, left alone, children will be more creative. Indeed, from his studies of children's artwork Brent Wilson (1992) concludes that, '...the child is the most conventional rather than the most creative producer of art' (p. 23). In the primary school years, although children may add more items to their figures, they are often reluctant to experiment further, at the same time becoming increasingly dissatisfied with their efforts. After the age of 9 or 10 years Betty Edwards (1979) has noted that many children are not at all enthusiastic about drawing, believing that they 'cannot draw' and are 'not artistic'. We should not, then, be afraid of popular cultural influences on children's work and, indeed, we have nothing to lose by encouraging them, since they apparently help to extend the range of images which children will adopt and experiment with.

Despite the criticisms the notion has persisted that children's artwork should be allowed to be uninhibited self-expression, without interference. Many teachers feel that the most they should or can do is to provide the materials and suggest interesting and exciting topics to inspire children's imaginations; a more directive approach is often frowned on as it might impose adult ways of drawing and painting and not allow the children to express and develop their own creativity. Although encouraging children with interesting topics and providing them with a range of materials is certainly to be applauded I don't believe that their artistic development or their self-expression and creativity will be stifled if we get more involved with what they are actually producing. After all, we don't leave children entirely to their own devices with music and writing; we think they need to be taught at least some basic techniques in order to express themselves.

Universal approaches to art education?

Approaches to art education are not universally the same. In contrast to those in the West, Chinese school children are taught in an extremely formal way right from the nursery and their artwork has been internationally acclaimed (*see Plates 3a & b*). Ellen Winner (1989) visited the People's Republic of China in the late 1980s and reported on the teaching techniques used there. I myself visited China in 1995 and what I saw was very similar to Winner's account. The way that the nurseries are organized is not markedly dissimilar from those in the West although the children do seem to be more disciplined. There is a marked difference in formality between the two cultures, however, when the Chinese children start grade school at age 6 years.

The children's day is strictly timetabled. They have one 40-minute art lesson per week taught by an art specialist. A lesson will have a clear topic and will be introduced by the teacher perhaps by showing the class some pictures or a video. As well as the topic itself there will also be an artistic 'point' to the lesson, such as the depiction of movement or the blending or contrast of colours.

Plate 3a 'My flying toy' by 5-year-old Zhang Xiao Chen.

Plate 3b *(page 85)* 'Hanging up the stars' by 6-year-old Han Yu Ze.

Figure 70: *(right)* The panda lesson in a Chinese school textbook.

While the teacher is introducing the topic the children will be expected to sit up straight with their hands behind their backs. If asked to respond a child will stand up to speak and will only sit down again when told to do so. Usually the topic will be continued the following week so that over a school term a child will complete ten pieces of work each of which will receive a mark and then the child will be awarded an average grade in art for the term.

Whatever the topic of the art lesson the teacher will spend some time in discussing the structure of the objects which the children might include in their pictures. For example, in a lesson I observed for 7-year-olds the teacher demonstrated the arm and leg movements for different sorts of swimming strokes. She also invited five or six children to draw figures on the blackboard while the rest of the class started on their own drawings. She then made various critical points about the figures drawn on the board and, in addition, she showed the children some pictures previously drawn by another class.

Each area of China has its own regional curriculum and text books and there are also textbooks for art, one for each grade level. The nature of these textbooks varies from region to region. In Nanjing, for example, the textbooks very much resemble the 'how to draw' books popular in the West (*see Figure 70*) whereas those in Beijing are more like source books, with reproduced examples of a variety of different ways in which well-known artists, both eastern and western, have treated the topic the children are currently studying. The children are encouraged to look closely at these pictures and are not discouraged from copying them.

Art has high status in China and parents encourage their children to become artists since it is a relatively high prestige occupation and also commands a government salary. At weekends an 'art school' occupies some of the ordinary primary school buildings in Beijing. Children between the ages of 4 and 14 can attend for half a day; there are far more pupils on the waiting lists than can be accommodated. The teachers are normally art teachers in schools or colleges or designers in industry and television; it is a privilege to be asked to join the weekend art school staff. Parents are very keen for their children to have this extra tuition in both eastern and western techniques of drawing and painting. The Chinese argue that unless the children are taught the basic techniques they have no means of giving expression to their ideas. They do not subscribe to the *laissez-faire* or 'leave them to it' approach; in fact, many teachers I met were horrified by this approach and believe that it must result in an undisciplined mess. They certainly do not consider that tuition will hamper creativity.

In Beijing I also met Du Mei, an art teacher who gives private lessons to children from the age of 3 years and whose pupils have

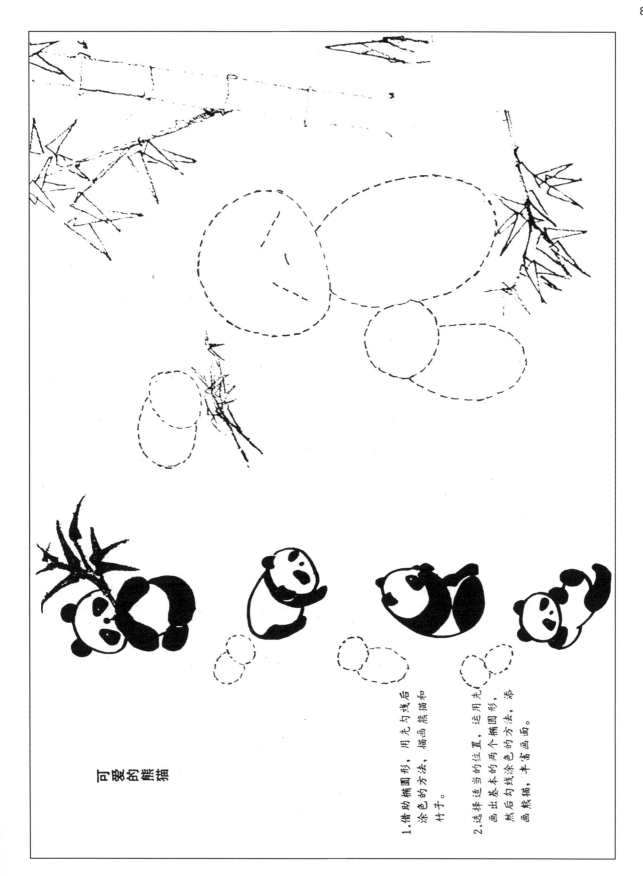

可爱的熊猫

1.借助椭圆形，用点勾线后涂色的方法，描画熊猫和竹子。

2.选择适当的位置，运用几画出基本的两个椭圆形的方法，添然后勾线涂色，丰富画面。画熊猫。

been very successful in national art competitions. Recently, some of her pupils have participated in a research project designed to assess the effectiveness of her teaching approach. The project is called 'Maximising the right half of the brain, developing the thinking of visualisation'. This reference to the right side of the brain relates to the idea that the mental processes associated with drawing skills are largely carried out in the right hemisphere of the brain. The reference also recalls Betty Edwards' (1979) useful book *Drawing on the Right Side of the Brain*.

Can we learn from the Chinese approach?

The Chinese approach to art may be far too formal for western tastes but I think we can at least learn something from it; in particular, we should not be shy of interacting with children while they are drawing and not always leave them to their own devices. We can do this in interesting and supportive ways; there doesn't have to be anything negative or critical about it and we don't have to impose a particular way of drawing on them. Probably one of the most important things we can do is to be interested and enthusiastic about artwork. Nearly all children will become interested in something which adults are interested in and excited about. Even better, if parents and teachers are seen to be doing some drawing and painting themselves then children will want to have a go too. Too often, art materials are set up for the children and they are expected simply to 'get on with it'. Far too infrequently do we see adults joining in; on the contrary, we often hear comments such as 'I'm no good at drawing' , 'I don't know anything about art'. These negative comments are hardly likely to encourage the child. In fact, they may suggest to the child that 'art' is a very specialized skill which only a very few adults, called 'artists', seem to have; furthermore, children may even get the message that art is a 'gift' which you either have or you haven't and that it is not something that can be learned.

First steps to teaching children to draw

My first recommendation, then, is that parents and teachers should not treat art simply as a 'filler activity' (Hargreaves and Galton, 1992), used to keep some children occupied while the adult attends to something considered more important elsewhere. Of course, that's not to say that children should never have time on their own to pursue their own ideas and artistic endeavours, but it is through frequent engagement with adults that children will become more interested and skilful. Normally, children do not see adults creating pictures. The pictures that they do see have usually been created by 'real artists' and are the finished products; the children have had no experience of seeing an artist at work. Indeed, they may have erroneous ideas about the process of creating a picture, believing for example that the work is effortless and is accomplished quickly and without erasure and alteration. The recent trend of inviting artists to work with children in schools is helping to dispel these beliefs; children come to appreciate that the artist is not simply and effortlessly churning out already practised images but is grappling with representational problems that makes the enterprise interesting and challenging.

Teachers can draw alongside the children

Of course, not all schools and nurseries can afford to invite artists to work with the children, especially when their budgets are very limited and there are so many other demands. But I believe that by engaging in the artistic activity themselves teachers (and parents) can go a long way towards stimulating the child's interest. When I was a primary school teacher I always worked on my own picture of the same topic I had set the rest of the class. I did not claim anything special for my ability as an artist but neither did I denigrate it unduly; certainly, I found that the shared activity stimulated the children's interest and generated discussion about what we were all trying to explore and achieve in our pictures.

Exploring crayon and paint

Very young children, even before their first birthday, may want to begin to explore the possibilities of crayon and paint. Of course, parents and nursery teachers may be concerned about the mess but as long as the children are coming to no harm there is no reason why they should not become acquainted with the materials at this very young age. It is often assumed that young children lack the coordination and control to make fine movements and that it will therefore be easier for them to use thick paintbrushes, crayons and pencils. Although they may enjoy the bold productions they make with these materials it is surprising how detailed their work can be as they learn to master finer implements and what satisfaction they gain from this achievement.

Imitating and copying

Children who have begun to scribble may be interested in the different kinds of scribble it is possible to produce. You can show them the various ways that lines can go: straight lines in different directions, wavy lines, zig-zagging lines, loopy lines, spirals, and so on. They can try to imitate these on the same page. It doesn't matter

Figure 71: Adult's zig-zag (left), loopy (upper middle) and straight line (upper right) scribbles. Amy's responses (centre) at age 1 year 1 week. (Drawn on lined paper.)

that they may not be able to copy your marks exactly or that their supposedly different scribbles actually all look very similar. They will begin to understand that it is at least possible to do a variety of things with the same crayon. In Figure 71, I demonstrated some zig-zags and some straight and loopy scribbles to my daughter Amy, aged 1 year and 1 week, and she was very keen to join in. These kinds of activity are probably best done with one child at a time as she may want to draw on your piece of paper rather than on a separate piece. Indeed she may choose to make her own drawing directly on top of yours. When I demonstrated a circular scribble to

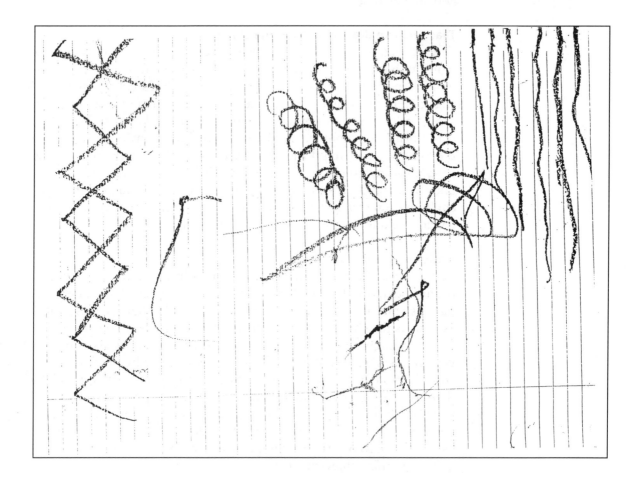

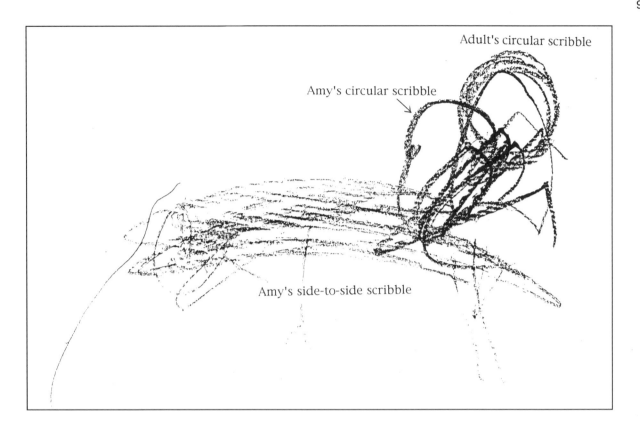

Adult's circular scribble

Amy's circular scribble

Amy's side-to-side scribble

Figure 72: At nearly 20 months, Amy produced side-to-side scribbles (centre) but could also attempt to copy an adult's circular scribble (right).

Amy, aged almost 20 months, her response was well targeted and a much more tightly circular scribble (*see Figure 72*) than her more usual widely sweeping movements.

Thinking about shapes

You can encourage slightly older children to think about shapes: curving a line and then making the ends join up to form a rough kind of circle. Experiment with other shapes too, although young children may well have difficulties in forming some of them, particularly a square or a triangle. Never the less, they will be interested in these games; they will have a go and be thrilled to find that adults like to get involved too.

Starting them off

Even if they have not yet drawn a recognizable figure children may be able 'help out' if we start them off. For example, you can draw a head and a body and then invite the child to suggest which other features she might add or simply tell her which parts you would like her to draw. Shortly before her second birthday Amy added a hat, some arms and some legs to the figure I had started for her (*see Figure 73*). The hat is a curved scribble around the head, the arms are formed from a horizontal side-to-side scribble and vertical

Figure 73: Amy, aged 1 year 11 months, added a hat, some arms and some legs to a pre-drawn head and body.

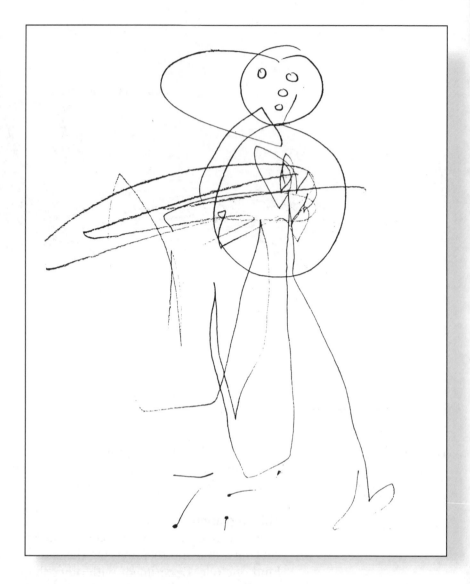

strokes are used for the legs. So, the scribbles may not look very realistic but neither are they random: they are targeted at the relevant parts of the figure and they also bear some resemblance to the parts they are meant to represent. Even when they can draw their own figures children still like to 'finish off' the incomplete figures we draw for them.

When children begin to draw figures of their own accord, however rudimentary, we can ask them to say which body part each line or shape represents. We might also suggest, or ask the children to suggest, other parts which have been missed out. In some cases these can easily be added. Shortly before her third birthday Amy drew a figure with legs but no feet and no arms. When her father suggested that she add these additional features she readily did so

Figure 74: Amy, aged almost 3 years, drew her figure sideways on the page, starting with the body. She added the feet and arms at her father's suggestion.

(*see Figure 74*). If children are still drawing tadpole figures some parts, such as the torso, are very difficult to add once the legs have been attached. We can encourage them to focus on the torso by asking them to draw another person, this time with 'a great big tummy'. We can also ask them to try beginning their drawing with the body rather than the head.

The 'dictation game'

Another task that children enjoy is the 'dictation game': dictate each part of the figure to the child before she is about to draw it. If you name more body parts than the child usually includes in her figures she is likely to draw something more elaborate and she also has to think about how she is going to draw each new part. (*See Figures 75 and 76.*) Not all children are prepared to draw every part we name; some tadpole-drawers, for example, may well ignore the body or even draw it separately at the side of the page! A variation on this game is to start the dictation with the legs or the body instead of the head.

Whether children are normally drawing tadpole figures or have started to draw a conventional figure they often enjoy being asked to draw 'contrasts' – for example, a girl and a boy or a little boy and a grown-up man (*see Figure 77*). This game gives children an opportunity to think about ways of adding to or adapting their figures in order to display their individual differences. In turn, this encourages them to be more adventurous in making their figures more varied instead of repeating the same formula each time.

Drawing different views

Although young children nearly always draw their figures facing the viewer they can be very interested in the idea of drawing other views – a view from the side or from the back (*see Figure 49*). This can be done from imagination or with one child acting as a model; dolls or small figures can be used as models too. The figures may be standing still and they can also appear to be walking or running. Again, this game encourages children to think about ways of adapting their drawings to reflect the different activities the figure might be engaged in. Above all it is important and useful to *talk* to children about their drawings, not only about the content (what each bit is meant to be) but also the problem of *how* you give the impression that someone is turning to the side or running in a race.

Figure 75: *(top)* Girl's 'free' drawing (left) and drawing from dictation (right); age 3 years 11 months.

Figure 76: *(middle)* Girl's free drawing (left) and drawing from dictation (right) in which the body was mentioned first and then the head; age 3 years 4 months

Figure 77: *(bottom)* 'A little boy and a grown-up man' by Katie, aged 3 years 10 months.

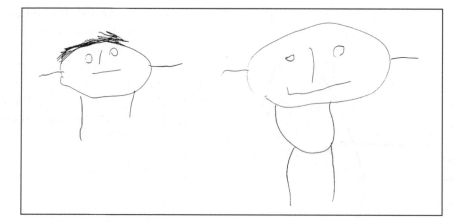

Drawing groups of people

In the main, I have discussed children's drawings of individual figures, but of course children enjoy drawing pictures which may include a number of people – the family, a group of friends playing, a birthday party, and so on. If they have had no experience of varying the way that they draw their figures young children may simply repeat their 'figure formula' (*see Figure 43*). In fact, this kind of exercise can form the basis of a discussion about how they might alter their figures so that there is more variation; as well as making the hairstyles different and adding different kinds of clothing they might also try to alter the postures and orientation of the figures. Whereas younger children are likely to draw a line of figures or dot them around the page older ones might be interested in other kinds of

Figure 78: *(top)* 'Ring-a-ring-a-Roses' by Melissa, aged 4 years 3 months; the figures are drawn in a line.

Figure 79: *(bottom)* 'Ring-a-ring-a-Roses' by Alice, aged 4 years 4 months; she has captured the idea of a circular game.

composition. You can stimulate their imaginations by suggesting they draw a children's game such as 'Pass the Parcel', 'Ring a ring a Roses' or 'The Farmer's in his Den', games in which the participants typically arrange themselves in a circle. (*See Figures 78 and 79.*)

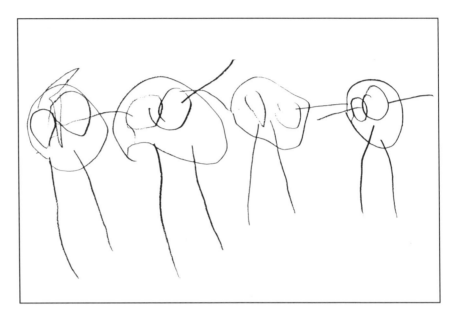

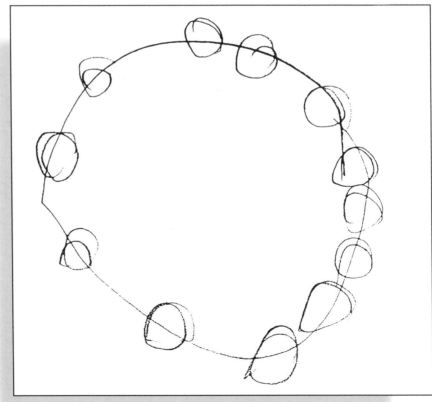

Exciting events

Children will also be keen to draw figures engaged in various events which are unusual and dramatic. During a snowy winter when my daughter, Amy, was 4 years 3 months I found it easier to pull both her and the shopping on a sledge through the streets. She loved it and, when we arrived home, immediately wanted to draw the experience. The picture was quickly executed with a wax crayon. First, she drew the sledge with herself and the shopping bag on it. And then, since the sledge took up most of the room on the page, her figure of me had to be crammed into the remaining space to the right-hand side. (*See Figure 80.*) Note that this figure of me has arms and hands to pull the ropes of the sledge but that the figure of

Figure 80: 'Mummy pulling me along on a sledge' drawn by Amy, aged 4 years 3 months.

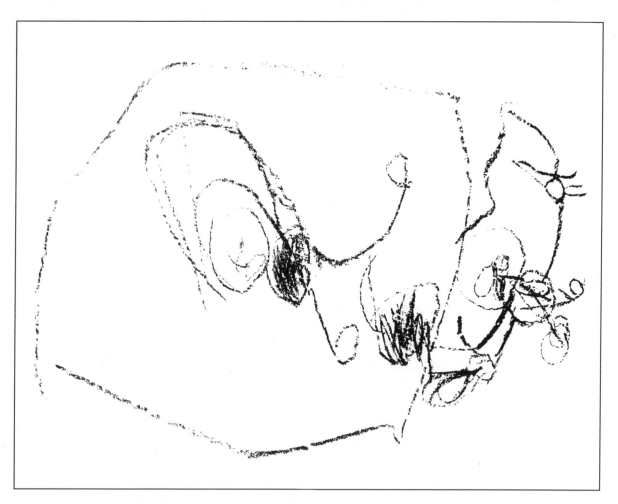

Figure 81: The 'negotiated drawing' approach to teaching children how to draw.

Amy has no arms at all; the curved lines around her head represent the hood of her coat. As I have noted before, children will not necessarily always make the most detailed and neat figure that they are capable of. If they are trying out a new posture or activity then it is not surprising that their figures will look less polished and more experimental.

Getting involved in children's picture-making

I appreciate that some people might feel uncomfortable with the idea of parents and teachers getting as involved in children's picture-making to the extent that I have advocated. Yet I do not consider that my suggestions will constrain the child's creative efforts and there is in fact some research evidence in support of this claim. Recently, I have been involved in evaluating an approach to teaching drawing in the infants school which incorporates discussion and careful observation of objects (Cox, Eames and Cooke, 1994). This approach, called the 'negotiated drawing' process, was developed by Grant Cooke, a former advisory art teacher, with the help of Deirdre Griffin, and although it was developed with 5- to 7-year-olds in mind the same principles could be used with slightly younger children and indeed with older ones.

Choosing a topic
Any topic, realistic or fantasy, might be chosen as the basis for an art activity. Those in our study included 'Frying an egg', 'The skeleton who can't dance' and 'Catching a dinosaur without hurting it'. Whatever the topic, the activity involves the children being asked to help the teacher to draw particular objects. I'll take the 'dancing skeleton' topic as an example. First of all the teacher fixes an

inflated plastic skeleton on or very near a blackboard. The children sit as close as they can so that they can all get more or less a similar view. The conversation between the teacher and the group might go as follows. (This example was first published in Cox, Cooke and Griffin, 1995.)

> *Teacher:* Can you help me draw this skeleton? It's going to be my hand which does the drawing, but your eyes and brains which tell my hand what to do. Should I start at the head or the body?

Sometimes the choice is completely open but, in this case, there is a chance that a child sitting at the front may choose a part of the skeleton which is too small to provide a good example at the start of the exercise. For this reason, the teacher poses a question which limits choice.

> *Child:* Head!
> *Teacher:* What shape is the head?
> *Child:* A circle.

In fact the skeleton's head is not a perfect circle, but the teacher takes the child's suggestion and draws a circle near the bottom of the board.

> *Child:* It's too low!
> *Teacher (asking the whole group):* What's wrong with that?
> *Child:* There's no room for the body.

This 'mistake' made by the teacher shows that even the first marks we make on a picture have to be thought about. The teacher rubs out the original circle and draws a very large circle near the top of the board, again rubbing it out when the children complain that it is too big and replacing it with a smaller circle.

> *Teacher:* Is this a proper circle?

The children start to describe the shape of the skeleton's head as an 'oval' or 'like an egg'. Following this new advice, the teacher makes the lower part of the head narrower.

> *Teacher:* I don't want to draw in the eyes and mouth now – when you do your drawings you can add those things.

The teacher judges that these things are too easy for her particular group and wants to move on to other parts of the body. The

children are invited to concentrate on the neck. (*See Figure 81.*)
Then they give instructions about how to draw the shape of the rib
cage.

> *Child:* It's square.

The teacher draws a very small square.

> *Child:* No. It's bigger.

The teacher rubs out the first square and draws another which is
too big.

> *Child:* No... It's sort of in between...

Eventually the children decide that the corners of this square should
be rounded. Quite often the teacher has to insist on moving on
otherwise the children can become obsessed about very small
features. When this happens she points out that the children will be
able to include all these details in their own drawings.

When the group focuses on the pattern of ribs painted on the
inflated skeleton the teacher uses an analogy.

> *Teacher:* Look, it is a bit like curving branches on a tree
> (pointing to a rib curving away from the breastbone). Can you
> hold your fingers up and make that shape in the air?

Asking the children to make a shape in this way is useful for
involving every child, particularly when some might be more vocal
or dominating than others.

It is unnecessary for the teacher to complete the drawing. The point
of the exercise is to create a route towards the child's own drawings.
So, she sits the inflated skeleton in a chair and starts to tell a story,
'One day when the children come in from play they hear a sobbing
noise and see a skeleton sitting in a chair crying...' The teacher gets
one of the children to ask the skeleton why it is so unhappy. They
are told that it used to be a dancing skeleton but one day it woke up
and found that it had forgotten how to dance. The teacher suggests
that the children might teach it how to dance, so they get up and
show some of the ways they can dance.

When all this is finished the teacher erases her drawing from the
board and invites the children to make their own pictures of how
the skeleton was taught to dance. The plastic skeleton remains in
view so that the children can observe it as they do their drawings
(*see Figure 82*).

Figure 82: *(left)* 'Teaching the skeleton how to dance' by a 6-year-old boy (upper) and girl (lower).

The negotiated drawing approach

This activity includes a range of things – visual, verbal and gestural. The children have to observe objects, talk about them, make fine discriminations. Their imaginations are stimulated and the whole activity is also interesting and fun. Normally, when children are set a topic they have difficulty, not because they lack imagination but because they often have difficulty in drawing the objects. The negotiated drawing approach helps children to get over this problem by engaging with them in a structured but non-rigid way. The teacher gives them a helping hand, although she doesn't tell them exactly how to draw. This helps to boost their confidence and makes it easier for them to incorporate a difficult object into an imaginative picture.

In order to test the effectiveness of this approach Grant Cooke and I devised a set of ten lessons and arranged for them to be given to children in two infants schools. Grant Cooke himself gave them to two classes of children. He also trained a supply teacher who gave them to another two classes. Grant Cooke took two further classes and gave them the same topics but taught them in a 'traditional' way. Finally, two more classes were taught by their own class teachers. Before the programme of lessons started we checked that these four different groups of children were similar in age and general ability. We also asked all the children to draw some pictures for us; these were done individually by each child without any help. We asked three art advisers to judge them and, according to these judgments, the four groups of children did not differ in their drawing ability at this point.

At the end of the study we asked the art advisers to compare the children's drawings of some of the topics covered in the lessons. In addition, the children were asked individually to draw the same pictures again that they had drawn before the study began. Each adviser independently gave each picture a rating from 1 (meaning 'poor') to 5 (meaning 'excellent'); the advisers had no idea which group each picture belonged to. Even so, we found that the ratings given by the advisers were higher for the pictures drawn by the children who had been in the 'negotiated drawing' lessons compared with those in the traditional lessons. This was the case for the pictures drawn during the lessons themselves and also for the pictures that the children had drawn on their own at the end of the study. Figure 83 shows a child's drawing of a telephone before and after he had received the programme of 'negotiated drawing' lessons. The advisers gave the first drawing ratings of 1 or 2, but the second one received ratings of 3 or 4; the advisers did not know that the two drawings were produced by the same child nor that one was completed before the study began and the other at the end. The results of this research provide objective evidence, then, that the

Figure 83: A 6-year-old boy's drawing of a telephone before and after a programme of 'negotiated drawing' lessons.

negotiated drawing process actually works. Interestingly, it also shows that children will not only benefit during the special sessions themselves but that these beneficial effects will also carry over into their other drawing activities.

Quite often a child may be concerned to make his figure 'look right' but may complain when he cannot do it to his own satisfaction. If achieving some degree of visual realism is the child's goal then I believe we should respect that and help him to achieve it. We do not have to dictate the way the figure should be drawn nor does our tutoring have to be so rigid that the child is indoctrinated into a particular way of drawing. But, our interest, enthusiasm and discussion of the problem can inspire the child to persevere and gain delight and satisfaction in the exercise. He is more likely to expand his repertoire of graphic images and be more confident in using and adapting these images in the future. The result should be a greater flexibility in his artistic productions.

Since this book has concentrated on children's drawings of the human figure it is not surprising that the concern has been largely about visual realism, about making the drawing 'look like' a human figure. But, of course, drawing, and art in general, is not only about producing recognizable images. Sometimes a child may have quite different concerns: although he may initially be inspired by a human figure he may be interested in its rhythm, its different component shapes or in its colour. And he may want to explore these aspects of the visual world in a purely abstract way with no intention of presenting the figure in a photographically realistic way or indeed in any representational way at all. So, it is important that we do not impose an idea of art that is solely an exercise in visual realism. It is much wider than that. But through our own involvement in art activities and in discussion we can motivate children, let them know that we think these activities are interesting and important and also help them to achieve more than they might otherwise do on their own. And, surely, that is what being a parent or a teacher is about.

Amelia Fysh

Amelia Fysh (née Bullen) was educated at the Wintringham Grammar School, Grimsby, and then from 1942– 46 served in the Royal Corps of Signals as a cypher operator and inspector. She trained as a teacher under the emergency training scheme after the Second World War, taught a reception class for two years and then a nursery class for a further five years. After attending a course in Child Development at London University's Institute of Education she became Head of Beech Green Nursery, Aylesbury, Buckinghamshire and remained there for seventeen years from 1956 to 1973 (*see Plate 4*).

It was during this period that Amelia Fysh and her staff pioneered the integration of handicapped children into the mainstream, long before the Warnock Report (1978) recommended this policy. Beech Green Nursery was selected to provide evidence to the Plowden Report (1967) on Primary Education. In 1972 a White Paper on 'nursery education for all' was put forward and Beech Green was constantly being visited by lecturers and advisers picking Amelia's brains. She was also regularly involved in planning and giving evening courses on Children and Provision for Play and was in particular demand to talk about the integration of handicapped children into mainstream nurseries. In 1973 she took up a post at the Margaret McMillan College of Education in Bradford, although her speaking engagements continued all around the country.

At Beech Green Nursery Amelia had started to collect folders of children's creative and imaginative work that she used for her own observation and as illustrations for her lectures. Despite the variation in the children's work she became aware that a developmental order seemed to exist and she wanted to discover more about it. She was particularly impressed with the work of Kenneth Jameson whose book *Pre-School and Infant Art* was published in 1968. Later, when Jameson became ill, Amelia took over some of his speaking engagements. In order to focus on the child's development of drawing Amelia concentrated on just one aspect, the 'draw a person' task, and with the cooperation of the nursery staff she was able to collect human figure drawings from the children throughout their stay in the nursery. Due to long waiting

Plate 4 Amelia Fysh at Beech Green Nursery where she was Head from 1956-73.

lists the children were of different ages when they first attended the nursery and some stayed longer than others. For some of them the sets of drawings are not very large but for others they span a period of 18 months or two years. Altogether, they cover the full range of social class backgrounds.

It was made clear to the children and the staff that this collection would be made by Amelia Fysh alone and only she would ask children to draw a picture for her special folder. All other work produced would be the children's own. The point of this distinction was to avoid any confusion of purpose either for the staff or the children themselves. The folder was always at hand – in a cupboard, on the top of the piano, on a trolley – with ready-cut pieces of paper and pencils or felt-tipped pens available. Amelia would never interrupt the children while they were absorbed in play or other activities but would catch them between activities or when they appeared to be 'at a loose end'. The instructions were simple: 'Draw a man, or a lady – a Mummy or Daddy, if you wish'. No questions were asked except 'Have you finished?', although any comments made by the child were noted down. No child was pressed to produce a figure if she didn't want to and, conversely, none was discouraged who wanted to produce more than one. The figures were dated and then mounted in sets when the children moved on from the nursery. This was a time-consuming task and two mothers helped with this work. Indeed, Amelia pays tribute to the kindness, generosity and support of the parents and the loyalty and diligence of her staff and ancillary helpers throughout her years at Beech Green. They all shared her interest and concern for the children and the children themselves spurred everyone on in the difficult days in an old building and the stimulating move to their new one.

Amelia Fysh's collection of human figure drawings is important for a number of reasons. To begin with, it is *longitudinal*: each child drew a series of figures over the period of time he or she attended the nursery. The collection was amassed over a nine-year period from 1964 to 1973. In many cases there are also follow-up drawings of 'my family', produced by the children when they were in the primary school. Longitudinal data are time consuming to collect and for this reason there are few studies of this kind in the research literature. A second important aspect of the collection is that the children are pre-schoolers; much research has been carried out with older children but the younger ones have attracted less attention. Thirdly, the size of the collection is notable: drawings were collected from 299 children. Fourthly, some of these children were intellectually impaired or had learning difficulties, physical disabilities or emotional disturbances or had disadvantaged or disrupted home backgrounds.

Amelia Fysh's collection was not intended as an academic or research-orientated piece of work. It did not set out to resolve specific questions or theories of child development. She was first and foremost a practising teacher committed to the needs of her children and in the provision of a climate for growth and development within the setting of a nursery school. It turns out, however, that the collection is a very valuable data base for researchers, lecturers and teachers concerned with young children's development in general as well as in their artistic and creative development. It is now in the National Arts Education Archive, Bretton Hall, University of Leeds.

References

Alland, A. (1983) *Playing with Form*. New York: Columbia University Press.

Ames, L.B. and Ilg, F.L. (1963) The Gesell incomplete man test as a measure of developmental status. *Genetic Psychology Monographs*, 68, pp. 247-307.

Arazos, A. and Davis, A. (1989) Young children's representation of gender in drawings. Presented at the British Psychological Society's Developmental Section Annual Conference, University of Surrey, September.

Archer, R.P., Maruish, M., Imhof, E.A. and Piotrowski, C. (in press) Psychological test usage with adolescent clients: 1990 survey findings. *Professional Psychology: Research and Practice*.

Arnheim, R. (1974) *Art and Visual Perception: A Psychology of the Creative Eye. The New Version*. 2nd edition. Berkeley, Los Angeles: University of California Press.

Barnes, E. (1894) The art of little children. *Pedagogical Seminary*, 3, pp. 302-307.

Bee, H. (1995) *The Developing Child*. 7th edition. New York: Harper Collins.

Bender, L. (1938) *A Visual Motor Gestalt Test and its Clinical Use. Research Monographs No. 3*. New York: American Orthopsychiatric Association.

Bradbury, R.J. and Papadakis-Michaelides, E. (1990) Gender differences in children's human figure drawings. Presented at the IVth European Conference on Developmental Psychology, University of Stirling, August.

Briggs, F. and Lehmann, K. (1989) Significance of children's drawings in cases of sexual abuse. *Early Child Development and Care*, 47, pp. 131-147.

Burt, C. (1921) *Mental and Scholastic Tests*. London: King & Son.

Cox, M. (1992) *Children's Drawings*. Harmondsworth, Middx.: Penguin Books.

Cox, M.V. (1993) *Children's Drawings of the Human Figure*. Hove, UK & Hillsdale, USA: Lawrence Erlbaum.

Cox, M.V., Cooke, G. and Griffin, D. (1995) Teaching children to draw in the Infants School. *Journal of Art & Design Education*, 14, pp. 153-163.

Cox, M.V., Eames, K. and Cooke, G. (1994) The teaching of drawing in the infants school: an evaluation of the 'negotiated drawing' approach. *International Journal of Early Years Education*, 2, pp. 68-83.

Cox, M.V. and Howarth, C. (1989) The human figure drawings of normal children and those with severe learning difficulties. *British Journal of Developmental Psychology*, 7, pp. 333-339.

Cox, M.V. and Moore, R. (1994) Children's depictions of different views of the human figure. *Educational Psychology*, 14, pp. 427-436.

Cox, M.V. and Parkin, C. (1986) Young children's human figure drawing: cross-sectional and longitudinal studies. *Educational Psychology*, 6, pp. 353-368.

Di Leo, J. (1970) *Young Children and Their Drawings*. New York: Brunner/Mazel.

Di Leo, J. (1973) *Children's Drawings as Diagnostic Aids*. New York: Brunner/Mazel.

Earl, C.J.C. (1933) The human figure drawing of feeble-minded adults. *Proceedings of the American Association of Mental Deficiency*, 38, pp. 107-120.

Edwards, B. (1979) *Drawing on the Right Side of the Brain*. Los Angeles: Tarcher.

Eng, H. (1931) *The Psychology of Children's Drawings*. London: Routledge & Kegan Paul.

Goh, D.S. and Fuller, G.B. (1983) Current practices in the assessment of personality and behavior by school psychologists. *School Psychology Review*, 12, pp. 240-243.

Golomb, C. (1981) Representation and reality: the origins and determinants of young children's drawings. *Review of Research in Visual Art Education*, 14, pp. 36-48.

Golomb, C. and Barr-Grossmann, T. (1977) Representational development of the human figure in familial retardates. *Genetic Psychology Monographs*, 95, pp. 247-266.

Goodenough, F. (1926) *Measurement of Intelligence by Drawings*. New York: Harcourt, Brace & World.

Goodnow, J. (1977) *Children's Drawing*. London: Fontana/Open Books.

Goodnow, J.J., Wilkins, P. and Dawes, L. (1986) Acquiring cultural forms: cognitive aspects of socialization illustrated by children's drawings and judgments of drawings. *International Journal of Behavioral Development*, 9, pp. 485-505.

Gridley, P.F. (1938) Graphic representation of a man by four-year-old children in nine prescribed drawing situations. *Genetic Psychology Monographs*, 20, pp. 183-350.

Hargreaves, D.J. and Galton, M.J. (1992) Aesthetic learning: psychological theory and educational practice. In Reimer, B. and Smith, R.A. (Eds.) *The Arts, Education and Aesthetic Knowing. 91st Yearbook of the NSSE. Part II*. Chicago: University of Chicago Press.

Harris, D.B. (1963) *Children's Drawings as Measures of Intellectual Maturity: A Revision and Extension of the Goodenough Draw-a-Man Test*. New York: Harcourt, Brace & World.

Hibbard, R.A., Roghmann, K. and Hoekelman, R.A. (1987) Genitalia in children's drawings: an association with sexual abuse. *Pediatrics*, 79, pp. 129-136.

Hurst, V. (1991) *Planning for Early Learning*. London: Paul Chapman.

Israelite, J. (1936) A comparison of the difficulty of items for intellectually normal children and mental defectives on the Goodenough drawing test. *American Journal of Orthopsychiatry*, 6, pp. 494-503.

Jameson, K. (1968) *Pre-School and Infant Art*. London: Studio Vista.

Kahill, S. (1984) Human figure drawing in adults: an update of the empirical evidence, 1967-1982. *Canadian Psychology*, 25, pp. 269-292.

Kellogg, R. (1970) *Analyzing Children's Art*. Palo Alto, Calif.:Mayfield.

Kerschensteiner, D.G. (1905) *Die Entwickelung der zeichnerischen Begabung*. Munich: Gerber.

Klopfer, W.G. and Taulbee, E.S. (1976) Projective tests. *Annual Review of Psychology*, 27, pp. 543-567.

Koppitz, E. (1968) *Psychological Evaluation of Children's Human Figure Drawings*. New York: Grune & Stratton.

Löwenfeld, V. (1939) *The Nature of Creative Activity*. New York: Macmillan.

Löwenfeld, V. (1957) *Creative and Mental Growth*. 3rd edition. New York: Macmillan.

Luquet, G-H. (1913) *Les Dessins d'un Enfant*. Paris: Alcan.

Luquet, G-H. (1920) Les bonhommes têtards dans le dessin enfantin. *Journal de Psychologie Normale*, 17, pp. 684-710.

Machover, K. (1949) *Personality Projection in the Drawings of the Human Figure*. Springfield, Il.: C.C. Thomas.

Major, D.R. (1906) *First Steps in Mental Growth*. New York: MacMillan.

Matthews, J. (1984) The young child's early representation and drawing. In Blenkin, G. and Kelly, A.V. (Eds.), *Early Childhood Education: A Developmental Curriculum*. London: Paul Chapman.

McElwee, E.W. (1934) Profile drawings of normal and subnormal children. *Journal of Applied Psychology*, 18, pp. 599-603.

Motta, R.W., Little, S.G. and Tobin, M.I. (1993) The use and abuse of human figure drawings. *School Psychology Quarterly*, 8, pp. 162-169.

Naglieri, J.A. (1988) *Draw a Person: A Quantitative Scoring System*. San Antonio, Texas: The Psychological Corporation, Harcourt Brace Jovanovich.

Papadakis-Michaelides, E.A. (1989) Development of Children's Drawings in Relation to Gender and Culture. Unpublished PhD thesis, University of Birmingham.

Piaget, J. and Inhelder, B. (1956) *The Child's Conception of Space*. London: Routledge & Kegan Paul.

Plowden Report. (1967) *Children and their Primary Schools. Report of the Central Advisory Council for Education (England)*. London: HMSO.

Prout, H. (1983) School psychologists and social-emotional assessment techniques: patterns in training and use. *School Psychology Review*, 12, pp. 377-383.

Ricci, C. (1887) *L'Arte dei Bambini*. Bologna: N. Zanichelli.

Roback, H.B. (1968) Human figure drawings: their utility in the psychologist's armamentarium for personality assessment. *Psychological Bulletin*, 70, pp. 1-19.

Rosen, A. and Boe, E. (1968) Frequency of nude figure drawings. *Journal of Projective Technique and Personality Assessment*, 32, pp. 483-485.

Rouma, G. (1913) *Le Language Graphique de l'Enfant*. Paris: Misch & Thron.

Schuyten, M.C. (1904) De oorspronkrlijke 'Ventjes' der Antwerpsch Schoolkindern. *Paedologisch Jaarboek*, 5, pp. 1-87.

Sitton, R. and Light, P. (1992) Drawing to differentiate: flexibility in young children's human figure drawings. *British Journal of Developmental Psychology*, 10, pp. 25-33.

Spoerl, D.T. (1940) The drawing ability of mentally retarded children. *Journal of Genetic Psychology*, 57, pp. 259-277.

Swensen, C.H. (1957) Sexual differentiation on the Draw-a-Person test. *Journal of Clinical Psychology*, 11, pp. 37-40.

Swensen, C.H. (1968) Empirical evaluations of human figure drawings. *Psychological Bulletin*, 54, pp. 431-466.

Viola, W. (1936) *Child Art and Franz Cizek. Vienna: Austrian Junior Red Cross.*

Warnock, M. (1978) *Special Educational Needs. Report of the Committee of Enquiry into the Education of Handicapped Children and Young People.* London: HMSO.

Willsdon, J.A. (1977) A discussion of some sex differences in a study of human figure drawings by children aged four-and-a-half to seven-and-a half-years. In Butterworth, G. (Ed.), *The Child's Representation of the World.* New York: Plenum Press.

Wilson, A. (1993) Children's drawings: more than just pretty pictures? *Top Santé Health and Beauty*, September, pp. 36-39.

Wilson, B. (1992) Primitivism, the avant-garde and the art of little children. In Thistlewood, D. (Ed.) *Drawing Research and Development.* Harlow, Essex: Longman/NSEAD.

Wilson, B. and Wilson, M. (1977) An iconoclastic view of the imagery sources in the drawings of young people. *Art Education*, 30, pp. 4-12.

Wilson, B. and Wilson, M. (1984) Children's drawings in Egypt: cultural style acquisition as graphic development. *Visual Arts Research*, 10, pp. 13-26.

Winner, E. (1989) How can Chinese children draw so well? *Journal of Aesthetic Education*, 22, pp. 17-34.

Index

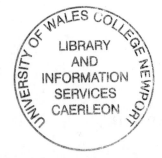